THE LITTLE GIANT® BOOK OF Baseball Facts

Michael J. Pellowski

Sterling Publishing Co., Inc.
New York

Dedication
To Kevin Liss & Ricky Gilchrist

Library of Congress Cataloging-in-Publication Data Available

10 9 8 7 6 5 4 3

Published by Sterling Publishing Co., Inc.
387 Park Avenue South, New York, NY 10016
© 2007 by Michael J. Pellowski
Distributed in Canada by Sterling Publishing
c/o Canadian Manda Group, 165 Dufferin Street
Toronto, Ontario, Canada M6K 3H6
Distributed in the United Kingdom by GMC Distribution Services
Castle Place, 166 High Street, Lewes, East Sussex, England BN7 1XU
Distributed in Australia by Capricorn Link (Australia) Pty. Ltd.
P.O. Box 704, Windsor, NSW 2756, Australia

Manufactured in China
All rights reserved.

Sterling ISBN-13: 978-1-4027-4273-6
       ISBN-10: 1-4027-4273-8

For information about custom editions, special sales, premium and
corporate purchases, please contact Sterling Special Sales
Department at 800-805-5489 or specialsales@sterlingpub.com.

Contents

Introduction   5

1. Up First!   8

2. Baseball is a Hit!   37

3. Let's Play Ball   68

4. Around the Infield   88

   In the First Place   89

   No Second Guessing   102

   Three is Not a Crowd   110

   Coming Up Shortstop   118

   Utility Work Ahead   124

5. In the Outfield   125

6. Here's the Pitch!   147

7. Let's Play Catch   181

8. Aye, Aye Skipper   197

9. Batter Up!   214

10. Kings of Clout   250

11. Take One for the Team   274

12. Pennants, All-Stars
       & the World Series   305

13. Touching All the Bases   323

14. The Last Inning   333

Index   338

About the Author   352

Introduction

Welcome baseball fans, young and old. Thanks for being part of America's favorite pastime. We're here at baseball's Fall Classic, the World Series. The annual competition between the champions of the National and American Leagues is deadlocked at three games each. It's the bottom of the ninth inning in the deciding game of the championship and the teams are knotted at six runs apiece. There are two outs and the bases are empty. The National League home team is down to its final out before extra innings. On the mound for the winners of the American League pennant is a young, hard-throwing, Cy Young Award winner. Facing him at the plate is the National League's home run hitting champ. It's a classic matchup of opposite league All-Stars.

The pitcher goes into his windup. He delivers his first pitch. It's a blazing fastball. The batter takes it and the umpire yells, "Strike one!" After the catcher tosses back the ball, the stocky hurler gets ready to throw again. He nods at the catcher's sign. Then, he delivers his next pitch to the plate. It's "Uncle Charlie," baseball slang for a curve ball. The batter takes a mighty swing and fouls it off into the stands where it becomes a treasured souvenir for some fortunate fan. "Strike two!" shouts the ump.

The count is now no balls and two strikes. The

pitcher does not want to waste a pitch. He wants to record a "K" which stands for a strike out. He throws another heater, his best fastball. The batter swings. There is a loud *crack* as the lumber connects with the speeding horsehide. Holy cow! There it goes. It's going, going, gone! The ball clears the outfield fence and lands in the opposing bullpen. It's a home run! The National League wins the World Series crown which was captured by the American League the year before.

What excitement! What drama! What a thrilling finish! This is Major League Baseball at its best! Here on these pages you'll find over 1,000 of baseball's best facts about amazing pennant races, astonishing pitching feats, astounding hitting achievements and much more. You'll marvel at super World Series moments and snicker at silly baseball slang, nutty player nicknames and crazy quotes. Now it's time for you to get in the game. So, let's play ball and read on!

CHAPTER 1
Up First!

It is not an easy job to lead off in baseball. The leadoff batter is usually the catalyst of important things to follow. What does it take to be a perfect leadoff guy? You have to be quick. You have to have a good eye for details. You have to know the game of baseball and be able to score for your team.

The quick-hitting facts you'll find in this chapter detail some of baseball's famous, fantastic, and funny firsts. After you read them, you'll know more about the great game of baseball from Little League to the Major Leagues. So, what's the score when it comes to who was up first in baseball? Start reading and find out.

In 2004, the Boston Red Sox won their first World Series since 1918. The Red Sox defeated the St. Louis Cardinals four games to none in the World Series to capture the championship.

◆

The first catcher's mask was worn in a baseball game in 1877 by Jim Tyng of the Harvard college team.

◆

In 1966, Emmett Ashford became the first African-American to umpire a Major League baseball game.

◆

Shortstop Derek Jeter of the New York Yankees hit his first Major League grand slam home run on June 18, 2005. Jeter's bases clearing blast came in an interleague game against the Chicago Cubs, which the Yankees won 8 to 1. The homer was Jeter's first grand slam in over eleven MLB seasons.

The 1891 baseball season was the first one in which teams were allowed to substitute for a player at any time in the game.

◆

Helen Britton was the first woman to own a Major League Baseball team. Ms. Britton took control of the St. Louis Cardinals in 1911.

◆

The Texas Rangers' first year in the American League was 1961.

◆

A unique baseball first occurred on July 14, 1972. On that day, Tom Haller was the catcher for the Detroit Tigers while his brother, Bill Haller, appeared in the same game as the home plate umpire.

When New York Mets batters Carlos Beltran, Carlos Delgado, David Wright, and Cliff Floyd homered in a game against the Washington Nationals on April 13, 2006, it was the first time in Mets history that the team's 3, 4, 5, and 6 hitters had all blasted home runs in the same game. The Mets won the contest 13 to 4.

◆

The Cincinnati Red Stockings were baseball's first all-professional team. The Red Stockings began play in 1869. They won 64 games without a single loss that season.

◆

In the game of baseball, the visiting team always bats first.

Mickey Mantle of the New York Yankees played his first Major League Baseball game on April 17, 1951. Mantle collected one hit in four at bats in the Yankees' 5 to 0 victory over the Boston Red Sox that day.

◆

The first no-hitter on record was pitched by Joe Borden of Philadelphia against Chicago in the National Association on July 28, 1875.

◆

In 1981, Steve Carlton became the first left-handed pitcher to record 3,000 career strikeouts.

◆

St. Louis pitcher Mark Mulder won the first game played at the new Busch Stadium, which opened April 10, 2006. The Cardinals beat the Milwaukee Brewers 6 to 4 in the game and Mulder contributed to the opening day celebration by hitting the first home run of his Major League career.

Albert Pujols of the St. Louis Cardinals won his first National League Most Valuable Player award in 2005. Pujols' statistics that season included a .330 batting average, 41 home runs, 195 hits, and 117 RBIs (RBIs).

◆

Al Leiter pitched the first no-hitter in Florida Marlins club history. On May 11, 1996, Leiter no-hit the Colorado Rockies as the Marlins recorded an 11 to 0 victory.

◆

The first baseball game played under artificial lights was held on September 2, 1880. The game took place between two Boston department store teams and occurred about a year after Thomas Edison first invented the electric light bulb.

◆

The first Negro League World Series in 1924 was won by the Kansas City Monarchs.

Catching Firsts

Johnny Bench of the Cincinnati Reds was the first catcher to win the National League Rookie of the Year Award, in 1968.

◆

The first time a chest protector was worn in baseball was in 1885.

◆

The first catcher with 500 at-bats in a single season was Connie Mack, in 1890.

◆

Thurman Munson of the New York Yankees was the first catcher to be named the American League Rookie of the Year, in 1970.

On July 17, 1990, the Minnesota Twins became the first team in Major League history to make two triple plays in a single game. Unfortunately for the Twins, they still lost the game to the Boston Red Sox 1 to 0.

◆

The Arizona Diamondbacks' first year in the National League was in 1998.

◆

New York Yankee Joe DiMaggio got the first hit in his record 56-game hitting streak on May 15, 1941. The hit was a single off of Ed Smith, a left-handed pitcher for the Chicago White Sox.

◆

Kirby Puckett of the Minnesota Twins was elected to the Baseball Hall of Fame in 2001 in his first year of eligibility.

On April 6, 1972, Major League Baseball's opening day games were cancelled for the first time due to a players' strike. The strike, which began on April 1, 1972, lasted for eighty-six games before it was settled.

◆

The first Little League baseball games were played in 1939.

◆

The Chicago White Sox were the first team to put players' names on their uniforms. They did it for the 1960 season.

◆

In 2005, Bartolo Colon became the first Los Angeles Angels pitcher to win the American League's Cy Young Award since 1964. Dean Chance, who captured the Cy Young Award in 1964, was the first Angels hurler in club history to be honored as the AL's top pitcher.

Jackie Robinson Fast Facts

In 1947, Jackie Robinson, a former star athlete at UCLA, became the first African-American to play in baseball's Major Leagues. Robinson played for the Brooklyn Dodgers.

Jackie Robinson's first position in the Major Leagues was at first base. He later played second base, third base, and outfield for the Dodgers.

Jackie Robinson was the first African-American to win baseball's Most Valuable Player Award, in 1949.

Jackie Robinson was the first African-American player inducted to the Baseball Hall of Fame, in 1962.

The first African-American pro baseball team was the New York-based Babylon Black Panthers in the 1880s.

◆

The first tripleheader in baseball history was played between the National League's Brooklyn Bridegrooms and the Pittsburgh Alleghenys on September 1, 1890, and host Brooklyn swept all three.

◆

Girls were permitted to officially participate in Little League baseball for the first time in 1974.

◆

The National Baseball Hall of Fame at Cooperstown, New York, was first opened in 1936.

◆

In 1996, Joe Torre guided the New York Yankees to a World Series championship in his first season as the Yankees' manager. New York beat the Atlanta Braves 4 games to 2.

The Cleveland Indians were the first baseball team to put numbers on their uniforms, in 1916. Indians' players wore numbers on their left sleeves for a few weeks. The practice of putting numbers on uniforms did not become a common practice until the early 1930s.

◆

The first fantasy baseball leagues were begun in 1980 by members of a New York literary community at a French restaurant, La Rotisserie Francaise. Fantasy baseball games use real-life statistics for fantasy teams created by a draft or auction.

◆

Carlos Baerga of the Cleveland Indians became the first player in Major League history to hit home runs from both sides of the plate in the same inning on April 8, 1993.

In the 2006 baseball season, Kenji Johjima of the Seattle Mariners became the first Japanese catcher to play in the Major Leagues.

◆

The first pitcher to record 300 wins in the 20th century was Christy Mathewson.

Ed Delahanty was the first player to win batting titles in both the National and American Leagues. In 1899, Delahanty won the NL batting crown with a .410 average. In 1902, he won the AL title by posting a .376 batting average.

◆

According to most baseball historians, the first pitcher to throw a curve ball was Arthur "Candy" Cummings, who played big league baseball in the 1860s.

◆

Alva "Bobo" Holloman of the St. Louis Browns pitched a no-hitter in his very first Major League start, against the Philadelphia Athletics on May 6, 1953.

◆

In 1902, shortstop George Davis of the Chicago White Sox became the first switch-hitter in baseball to collect 2,000 hits.

Pop Up Quiz

1. Who was the first Major League player to get twelve consecutive hits? Was it Walt Dropo or Mike Higgins?

◆

2. Which school won the first College Baseball World Series in 1947? Was it Texas, California, or Oklahoma?

◆

3. Who was the first player selected in the 1993 Major League Baseball Draft? Was it Chipper Jones or Alex Rodriguez?

Answers

1. Mike Higgins of the Boston Red Sox was the first player to collect twelve hits in a row, in 1938. Walt Dropo of the Detroit Tigers duplicated the feat in 1952.

◆

2. California, coached by Clint Evans, won the first College World Series over Yale 8 to 7.

◆

3. Alex Rodriguez was the first player selected in the 1993 MLB draft, picked by the Seattle Mariners. Chipper Jones was the first player picked in the 1990 draft, by the Atlanta Braves.

In 2005, the Chicago White Sox won the World Series, defeating the Houston Astros 4 games to 0 for their first World Series title since 1917.

◆

Ralph Kiner of the Pittsburgh Pirates was the first National League player to hit 50 home runs twice. Kiner blasted 51 round-trippers in 1947 and 54 dingers in 1949.

◆

Kelly Craig was the first female starting pitcher in Little League World Series history. On August 21, 1990, Craig pitched for Canadian champion Trail against Matamoros, of Mexico. Canada won the game 8 to 3.

◆

Major League Baseball was televised for the first time when WXBS TV brought cameras to Ebbets Field to broadcast a doubleheader between the Brooklyn Dodgers and the Cincinnati Reds on August 26, 1939.

The Kansas City Royals won the World Series for the first time in 1985 when they defeated the St. Louis Cardinals 4 games to 3.

◆

The first baseball All-Star game was played at Chicago's Comiskey Park on July 6, 1933. The American League topped the National League 4 to 2. Connie Mack managed the AL squad, and John McGraw the NL team.

◆

American Legion baseball first began in 1925.

◆

The first United States president to attend a Major League Baseball game was Benjamin Harrison, who watched Cincinnati beat Washington 7 to 4 on June 6, 1892. President William Howard Taft was first to throw out the first pitch on April 14, 1910, at a Washington Senators game.

Morgan G. Bulkeley was the first president of baseball's National League. He held his office in 1876 and served for only one year.

♦

The first president of the American League was Ban Johnson, who served from 1901 to 1927.

♦

Kenesaw Mountain Landis was Major League Baseball's first commissioner, from 1920 until he died in 1944.

♦

The first professional game in Boston's Fenway Park took place on April 20, 1912, when the Boston Red Sox beat the New York Highlanders 7 to 6 in 11 innings.

♦

The first five players elected to the Baseball Hall of Fame in 1936 were Ty Cobb, Christy Mathewson, Honus Wagner, Babe Ruth, and Walter Johnson.

The San Diego Padres' first year in the National League was 1969.

◆

Leroy "Satchel" Paige was the first African-American pitcher to play in the Major Leagues. Paige was a member of the Cleveland Indians pitching staff in 1948.

◆

Charles Waite, an outfielder with the St. Louis Browns, is believed to be the first player to use a baseball glove to catch the ball. Waite put on his crude mitt in 1875.

◆

The Colorado Rockies' first year in the National League was in 1993.

◆

Major League pitchers were allowed to use a resin bag to dry their hands on the mound for the first time in the 1925 season.

Throwing a spitball was first ruled illegal in the Major Leagues in 1920.

◆

Barry Bonds of the San Francisco Giants was the first player in Major League history to hit more than 70 home runs in a single season. Bonds blasted 73 fence-clearing round-trippers in 2001.

◆

Joe Morgan of the Cincinnati Reds was the first player in baseball history to steal 600 bases and hit 200 home runs.

◆

The infield fly rule was adopted by baseball in 1901. It was developed to prevent fielders from dropping easy pop-ups on purpose in order to turn them into double plays.

◆

Elston Howard was the first African-American baseball coach in the American League. Howard coached for the New York Yankees in 1969.

Third baseman Brooks Robinson was the first member of the Baltimore Orioles to be named the Most Valuable Player of the All-Star game, in 1966.

◆

Mel Ott of the New York Giants was the first big league manager to get ejected in both games of a doubleheader. On June 9, 1946, Ott was tossed out of back-to-back games against the Pittsburgh Pirates. Pittsburgh won both contests.

◆

In 1989, Victoria Brucker was the first American girl to play in the Little League World Series. Victoria was a member of a team from San Pedro, California.

In 1991, the Toronto Blue Jays became the first team in sports history to draw four million fans in a single season.

◆

Ike Brown of the Detroit Tigers homered in his first major league at bat on June 17, 1969, in a game against the New York Yankees.

◆

The first baseball game in Berlin, Germany was played on June 12, 1912. To call balls and strikes behind the plate, the umpire wore a medieval suit of armor.

◆

The Oakland Athletics franchise played their first games in 1901, when they were known as the Philadelphia Athletics.

Pitcher Joe Niekro of the Houston Astros played in over 300 Major League games before he hit his first big league home run. Niekro's first round tripper came on May 29, 1976, against the Atlanta Braves, off his brother Phil Niekro.

◆

The Tampa Bay Devil Rays made Delmon Young the first player picked in the 2003 major league draft.

◆

Pete Rose of the Cincinnati Reds tripled off pitcher Bob Friend of the Pittsburgh Pirates on April 13, 1963, to collect his first major league hit.

◆

In 1989, Betty Speziale became the first female umpire to officiate a Little League World Series game.

Babe Ruth Firsts

Babe Ruth hit his first major league home run in a game he was pitching for the Boston Red Sox at New York's Polo Grounds on May 6, 1915.

◆

On May 20, 1919, Babe Ruth of the Boston Red Sox hit the first grand slam of his major league career. Ruth's bases-clearing blast came in a 6 to 4 victory over the St. Louis Browns. Ruth was also the game's winning pitcher.

◆

Babe Ruth's first year with the New York Yankees was in 1920, when he belted 54 home runs.

◆

The first and only time Babe Ruth led the American League in batting was in 1924, when he posted a .378 average.

Tony Cloninger of the Atlanta Braves was the first National League pitcher to hit two grand slams in a game, on July 3, 1966, in a 17 to 3 rout of the San Francisco Giants.

◆

The first American League night game was between the Cleveland Indians and the Philadelphia Athletics at Philadelphia's Shibe Park on May 16, 1939.

◆

Gaylord Perry was the first major league pitcher to win Cy Young Awards in both the American and National Leagues. Perry won the AL Cy Young Award in 1972 as a hurler for the Cleveland Indians. In 1978, Perry won the NL Cy Young Award while pitching for the San Diego Padres.

◆

Jack McCarthy of the Chicago Cubs was the first outfielder in major league history to throw out three runners at home plate in a single game.

McCarthy nailed three Pittsburgh Pirates attempting to score on April 26, 1905.

◆

Robin Ventura of the New York Mets was the first major leaguer to hit grand slams in both games of a doubleheader. Ventura did it on May 20, 1999, against the Milwaukee Brewers.

◆

Baseball cards were issued for the first time around 1884. They were packed as prizes in cigar boxes and tobacco tins. Baseball cards were packaged with bubblegum for the first time in the 1930s.

Ty Cobb's first major league hit was a double. Cobb clubbed it off New York Highlanders pitcher Jack Chesbro on August 30, 1905. The Detroit Tigers beat the Highlanders 5 to 3 that day.

◆

Sparky Anderson of the Cincinnati Reds and the Detroit Tigers was the first manager to win more than 100 games in each league.

◆

Nomar Garciaparra's first RBIs as a member of the Los Angeles Dodgers came on a grand slam he belted off Houston Astros pitcher Brad Lidge on April 24, 2006.

◆

After coming to America from Japan, Kaz Matsui of the New York Mets hit a home run on the first pitch in his first at-bat in his first game in America's National League. The homer came in April 2004 off pitcher Russ Ortiz of the Atlanta Braves.

Willie Wilson of the Kansas City Royals was the first player in major league history to come to bat 700 times in a single season. In 1980, Wilson had 705 official at-bats.

◆

Jeremy Hermida of the Florida Marlins hit a pinch-hit grand slam off pitcher Al Reyes of the St. Louis Cardinals in his first major league at-bat on August 31, 2005.

◆

The use of batting helmets first became required in the National League in 1957. The American League first tried batting helmets in 1958, but they were not required by league rules until 1971.

◆

The Cincinnati Reds beat the Philadelphia Phillies 2 to 1 in the first night game played by two major league teams, on May 24, 1935 in Cincinnati.

CHAPTER 2
Baseball is a Hit!

Okay, hometown fans. It's time to stand up and cheer for your favorite player, team, or manager. All of the game's greats, past and present, from Ted Williams to Ivan "Pudge" Rodriguez are on deck and ready for you to review their super statistics, fantastic feats, and nutty nicknames. Go back in sports history to discover who, what, why, and when about the great game of baseball. Who were the Black Sox and how did they get their infamous name? When was the last game played at New York's old Polo Grounds? What number did the immortal Babe Ruth wear? You find the answers to those questions and much more as you circle the bases to record your first big league extra base hit.

Alexander Cartwright drew up the first official rules for the game of baseball in 1845. Cartwright's rules established foul lines, the strike out, three-out innings, nine-man teams, and a distance of ninety feet between bases.

◆

The teams in the East Division of the American League are the New York Yankees, the Boston Red Sox, the Toronto Blue Jays, the Baltimore Orioles, and the Tampa Bay Devil Rays.

◆

Baseball's first Bat Day was held in 1952 by the St. Louis Browns.

◆

The Arizona Diamondbacks, San Diego Padres, Colorado Rockies, Los Angeles Dodgers, and San Francisco Giants are the teams in the West Division of the National League.

The first legitimate pro baseball league was formed in 1871. It was called the National Association of Professional Baseball Players.

◆

Experts have calculated that the odds against a player completing an unassisted triple play in baseball are 50,000 to 1.

◆

The National League is the oldest baseball league still in operation. The National League was organized in 1875–76 from the National Association of Professional Baseball Players. The change allowed the NL to become a league of clubs instead of an association of players.

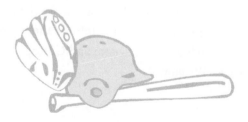

The first National League champions were the Chicago White Stockings, who took the pennant in 1876.

◆

The first Major League Baseball team to fly to an away game was the Boston Red Sox, who flew from a game in St. Louis to a game in Chicago on July 30, 1936.

◆

The teams in the East Division of the National League are the Atlanta Braves, New York Mets, Florida Marlins, Philadelphia Phillies, and Washington Nationals.

◆

The All-American Girls Professional Baseball League was founded in 1943 and was the brain-child of chewing gum magnate and Chicago Cubs owner P.K. Wrigley.

The baseball teams in the Central Division of the National League are the St. Louis Cardinals, Cincinnati Reds, Houston Astros, Milwaukee Brewers, Chicago Cubs, and Pittsburgh Pirates.

◆

Over five thousand years ago, ancient Egyptians had batting contests with crude clubs and balls.

◆

The National Association of Baseball Players printed baseball's first official rule book in 1858.

The last baseball game played at New York's Polo Grounds was on September 18, 1963. In the contest, the visiting Philadelphia Phillies beat the New York Mets 5 to 1. The Polo Grounds was demolished in 1964 to make room for a housing project.

◆

The Chicago White Sox, Detroit Tigers, Cleveland Indians, Minnesota Twins, and Kansas City Royals are the teams in the Central Division of the American League.

◆

The teams who were original members of the All-American Girls Professional Baseball League were the Rockford Peaches, the South Bend Blue Sox, the Racine Belles, and the Kenosha Comets.

◆

Before Columbus discovered America in 1492, Navajo Native Americans were playing a batting game with four bases. After hitting a ball with a stick, a Navajo batter ran from base to base trying to elude being caught by players in the field.

◆

Shortstop Ozzie Smith of the St. Louis Cardinals wore No. 1. Smith was nicknamed "The Wizard of Oz" because of his fielding ability.

◆

The baseball teams in the West Division of the American League are the Seattle Mariners, Texas Rangers, Oakland Athletics, and Los Angeles Angels.

◆

Frank Robinson of the Cincinnati Reds was Major League Baseball's first unanimous Rookie of the Year Award winner, in 1956.

A game similar to baseball was played in Britain in the 1700s. The game was called Rounders and in it wooden posts were used as bases. A batter hits the ball and tries to run around the bases. Players in the field try to "put out" the runner by hitting him with the ball.

◆

In 1879, pitcher Will White pitched 75 complete games and 680 innings. In 1877, he was the first player to wear eyeglasses in the major leagues.

◆

The All-American Girls Professional Baseball League folded in 1954.

◆

Larry Berra got the nickname "Yogi" while he was in school in St. Louis, Missouri. A friend said Berra reminded him of a Hindu fakir or a yogi. Berra's friends started calling him Yogi and the name stuck.

Infielder Ron Hunt was the first New York Met to be named a starter for the National League in the All-Star game. Batting .303, Hunt started for the 1964 NL All-Stars, who defeated the AL All-Stars 7 to 4 at Shea Stadium.

◆

In 1867, there were more than 400 teams in the National Association of Baseball Players.

◆

Baltimore pitcher Matt Kilroy struck out 513 batters in 68 games in 1886.

Number Quiz

Match each of the following big league players
with the number he wore:

1. Babe Ruth	A. No. 23
2. Barry Bonds	B. No. 9
3. Ichiro Suzuki	C. No. 21
4. Don Mattingly	D. No. 3
5. Carlos Delgado	E. No. 25
6. Ted Williams	F. No. 51

The correct answers are 1: D (Babe Ruth No. 3);
2: E (Barry Bonds No. 25); 3: F (Ichiro Suzuki No. 51);
4: A (Don Mattingly No. 23); 5: C (Carlos Delgado
No. 21); and 6: B (Ted Williams No. 9).

In 1901, the National League voted to make any foul ball not caught on the fly a strike unless the batter had two strikes on him. The American League adopted the same rule in 1903.

◆

Baseball announcer Joe Garagiola, who is a former major league catcher, was a childhood friend of Hall of Famer Yogi Berra in a working-class Italian-American section of St. Louis.

◆

The first organized baseball game between formal teams was played on June 19, 1846, in Hoboken, New Jersey. The teams were the Knickerbockers and the New York Nine. The New York Nine beat the Knickerbockers 23 to 1.

◆

Pitcher Nolan Ryan won 324 games during his career from 1966–93 and struck out 5,714 batters.

Stan Musial of the St. Louis Cardinals is one of Major League Baseball's greatest hitters. Musial began his career as a pitcher, and pitched in the minor leagues from 1938 to 1940. He injured his shoulder while making a diving catch and could not continue his pitching career, so he moved into the outfield. He pitched once for St. Louis in 1952.

♦

On May 4, 1975, Bob Watson of the Houston Astros scored the one millionth run in baseball history. Watson tallied the historic run against the San Francisco Giants on a three-run homer by teammate Milt May.

♦

Hall of Famer Lou Gehrig pitched and played first base in college for Columbia University In 1923.

Walter R. Johnson, who pitched for the Washington Senators in the early 1900s, was nicknamed "The Big Train." Johnson won 417 games on the mound from 1907–1927.

◆

There have been six leagues considered to be major baseball leagues since 1870. They are the old American Association, the Union Association, the Players League, the Federal League, the American League, and the National League.

◆

Pitcher Cy Young won 511 games in his 22-year career on the mound. He also struck out a total of 2,803 batters.

◆

Hack Wilson of the Chicago Cubs collected 191 RBIs in 1930, leading the National League.

Baseball batters were entitled to four strikes at the plate in 1887. The rule was changed back to three strikes in 1888.

◆

A fair ball caught on one bounce was an out in baseball from 1845 to 1863. The rule was changed in 1864.

◆

Joe Randa hit the first game-ending home run in 129 season openers for the Cincinnati Reds on April 4, 2005. Randa's opening day walk-off shot was a solo homer off New York Mets pitcher Braden Looper. The Reds won 7 to 6.

◆

Frank "Home Run" Baker of the Philadelphia Athletics got his nickname in the 1911 World Series against the New York Giants. Baker hit homers off Giants pitchers Christy Mathewson and Rube Marquard to help the Athletics win the Series 4 games to 2.

Rogers Hornsby of the St. Louis Cardinals posted a career-best .424 batting average in 1924. He batted .400 in four seasons.

◆

Pitcher Sandy Koufax of the Los Angeles Dodgers struck out 382 batters in the 1965 season.

◆

The St. Louis Cardinals were known as the St. Louis Perfectos in 1899.

◆

Scott Podsednik of the Chicago White Sox was the first player in Major League history to homer in the World Series without hitting a single home run during the regular season. On October 23, 2005, Podsednik clubbed a fence-clearing ball in the ninth inning off Houston Astros pitcher Brad Lidge. The historic home run gave Chicago a 7 to 6 victory in the second game of the Series, which the White Sox ended up winning.

Jack Chesbro won 41 games while pitching for the New York Giants in 1904.

◆

Hall of Fame pitcher Christy Mathewson played college baseball and football at Bucknell College in Pennsylvania.

◆

A foul ball caught on one bounce was counted as an out in baseball until 1883.

The Black Sox Scandal

In one of the most shameful incidents in the history of Major League Baseball, eight members of the Chicago White Sox were accused of taking bribes from gamblers to throw the 1919 World Series against the Cincinnati Reds.

The White Sox were a powerful team that combined good hitting and fielding with solid pitching. "Shoeless" Joe Jackson, George "Buck" Weaver, and Eddie Collins provided the hitting punch at the plate. Oscar "Happy" Felsch, Arnold "Chick" Gandil, and Ray Schalk played tough defense. Pitchers Eddie Cicotte, Claude "Lefty" Williams, and rookie hurler Dickie Kerr were kings of the hill on the mound. How good were the Chicago White Sox in those days? In 1917, the White Sox won the American League pennant by besting the Detroit Tigers led by Ty Cobb, the Cleveland Indians led by Tris Speaker, and the Boston Red Sox led by Babe Ruth. In the 1917 World Series, they easily defeated the New York Giants managed by John McGraw.

Charles Comiskey, the owner of the White Sox, promised his players a big bonus for winning the 1917 World Series, but never paid it. In fact, Comiskey paid his players very poorly, which sports experts believe led to them accepting bribes for losing the 1919 World Series to underdog Cincinnati. The eight Chicago players accused of taking bribes from groups of gamblers headed by Arnold Rothstein (a famous gangster) and Joe "Sport" Sullivan were Joe Jackson, Buck Weaver, Chick Gandil, Eddie Cicotte, Lefty Williams, Happy Felsch, shortstop

Charles "Swede" Risberg, and utility player Fred McMullin.

The charges against the eight players were never proven in court. However, Kenesaw Mountain Landis, baseball's first commissioner, banned all eight White Sox players from playing in the major leagues for life. Since the cloud of guilt was never completely erased, the 1919 Chicago White Sox became known as the Black Sox. The scandal prevented great players like Joe Jackson from being inducted into Baseball's Hall of Fame.

Bernie Williams of the New York Yankees wore No. 51. He recorded his 1,200th RBI against the Kansas City Royals on April 13, 2006.

◆

Craig Biggio of the Houston Astros, Mo Vaughn of the New York Mets, and pitcher Mat Morris of the San Francisco Giants all played college baseball at Seton Hall University in New Jersey.

◆

Sammy Sosa of the Chicago Cubs led the National League with 50 home runs in 2000, and 49 round-trippers in 2002.

◆

The Cleveland Spiders of the National League won only 20 games and lost 134 diamond contests during the 1899 season.

In baseball games before 1887, the batter had the right to call for a high or low pitch from the opposing pitcher.

◆

Nap Lajoie of the Cleveland Indians won the American League batting crown in 1904 with a .376 batting average. It was the fourth straight year he led the league.

◆

In 2004, the New York Yankees became the first Major League Baseball team to lose a championship series after winning the first three games of the best-of-seven series. The Yankees won the first three contests of the American League Championship Series and then lost four straight games to the Boston Red Sox to be eliminated.

◆

Centerfielder Ray Van Cleef of Rutgers University was voted the Most Valuable Player of the College World Series in 1950.

Nickname Game

Match each of the following players with his correct baseball nickname:

1. Lou Gehrig

2. Ty Cobb

3. Dom DiMaggio

4. Willie McCovey

5. Willie Mays

6. Willie Stargell

A. The Say Hey Kid

B. The Little Professor

C. The Iron Horse

D. The Georgia Peach

E. Stretch

F. Pops

The answers are: 1–C (Lou Gehrig—The Iron Horse); 2–D (Ty Cobb—The Georgia Peach); 3–B (Dom DiMaggio—The Little Professor); 4–E (Willie McCovey—Stretch); 5–A (Willie Mays—the Say Hey Kid); 6–F (Willie Stargell—Pops).

On August 9, 1988, the Chicago Cubs won the first official night game at Wrigley Field by defeating the New York Mets 6 to 4.

◆

Manny Ramirez of the Boston Red Sox was voted the Most Valuable Player of the 2004 World Series.

◆

Lou Gehrig of the New York Yankees hit four consecutive home runs on June 3, 1932.

◆

Harold "Pie" Traynor played 17 years as a third baseman for the Pittsburgh Pirates and had a .320 career batting average.

◆

Elmer Smith of the Cleveland Indians hit the first grand slam in World Series play. Smith clubbed a bases-loaded home run in the fifth game of the 1920 World Series against the Brooklyn Dodgers.

Jermaine Dye of the Chicago White Sox was voted the Most Valuable Player of the 2005 World Series.

♦

In 1905, the Detroit Tigers signed Tyrus Raymond Cobb to a contract. Ty Cobb is considered to be the greatest player in baseball history and the Tigers signed him for seven hundred dollars.

♦

Connie Mack, who managed the Pittsburgh Pirates (NL) and the Philadelphia Athletics (AL), won 3,776 games in his 53 years as a major league skipper.

♦

In 1950, Sam Jethroe became the first African-American player to play for the Boston Braves.

♦

Shortstop Khalil Greene of Clemson was the Baseball America Player of the Year in 2002.

In 1994, catcher Jason Varitek of Georgia Tech was the Baseball America Player of the Year.

◆

First baseman Todd Helton of Tennessee was named the Baseball America Player of the Year in 1995.

◆

Baseball pitchers delivered the ball underhanded to the plate until 1883.

◆

Joe DiMaggio of the New York Yankees was one of the most famous centerfielders in baseball history. For the first month of his major league career, he played right field.

◆

Bobby Cox became the manager of the Atlanta Braves in 1978. Cox was a third base coach with the New York Yankees in 1977. He was also a former third baseman for the Yankees as a player.

In 1879, a batter in the game of baseball was issued a walk after a pitcher threw nine balls.

In 1887, hitters walked to first base after the pitcher threw five balls.

It was not until 1889 that batters were allowed to go to first base after a pitcher threw four balls.

Henry Aaron of the Milwaukee Braves won his first National League home run crown in 1957, when he blasted 44 homers.

In 1887, a batter who was issued a walk was credited with a hit in the box score.

Statistics on stolen bases in baseball were not kept until 1886.

Catcher Ivan "Pudge" Rodriguez hit .297, blasted 16 home runs, and collected 85 RBI's as a member of the Florida Marlins in 2003.

Pitcher Dazzy Vance of the Brooklyn Dodgers led the National League in strikeouts from 1922 to 1928. Vance's best year was in 1924, when he fanned 262 opposing batters.

Eddie Matthews is the only player who saw action as a member of the Boston Braves, the Milwaukee Braves, and the Atlanta Braves.

Philadelphia's William Dugleby hit a grand slam in his first major league at-bat on April 21, 1890. Dugleby was the first person in major league history to accomplish that.

Ted Williams posted a .406 batting average as a member of the Boston Red Sox in 1941. Williams collected six hits in eight at bats in a doubleheader against the Philadelphia Athletics on the final day of the 1941 season to boost his .399 average over the .400 mark.

◆

Don Larsen of the New York Yankees pitched the first and only perfect game in World Series history. Larsen's gem came in the fifth game of the 1956 World Series against the Brooklyn Dodgers. He threw only 97 pitches to accomplish the feat. The last batter he faced was pinch-hitter Dale Mitchell, who struck out. The Yankees won 2 to 0.

◆

Jimmy Foxx of the Philadelphia Athletics won baseball's Triple Crown in 1933. Foxx led the American League with 48 home runs, 163 RBIs, and a .356 batting average.

On April 20, 2006, Julio Franco of the New York Mets hit a home run against the San Diego Padres. Franco, who was 47 years and 240 days old when he blasted his pinch-hit round-tripper, was the oldest player in major league history to ever hit a home run. The historic blast was hit off Padres reliever Scott Linebrink.

◆

Songwriter Jack Norworth, who composed the lyrics of the famous baseball tune, "Take Me Out To the Ball Game," wrote the song before he actually ever saw a game of professional baseball played. Norworth penned the ballpark tune in 1906. He did not personally attend a game until the year 1940.

◆

In August 1972, a minor league game in Midland, Texas, was cancelled because of bug infestation. Millions of grasshoppers invaded the stadium and swarmed all over the field, making play impossible.

In 1980, a Pacific Coast minor league game in Washington State was postponed due to ash from the Mount St. Helens volcanic eruption.

◆

Al Reach is believed to be baseball's first paid professional. Reach was paid a salary of $275 from a Philadelphia-based team in 1864.

◆

A baseball game between the Colorado Rockies and the San Diego Padres was halted and eventually postponed because of snow on April 14, 1999.

◆

Manager and ex-major leaguer Casey Stengel wore No. 37. Stengel's number has been retired by both the New York Yankees and the New York Mets.

◆

The Gold Glove Awards began in 1957. The awards are given to the top fielders at every position in each league.

The first professional minor league was the International Association, which was organized in 1877.

◆

The first college baseball game was played between Amherst College and Williams College on July 1, 1859. Amherst won by the score of 73 to 32 in 26 innings.

◆

In the early days of baseball, balls hit into the stands were expected to be returned to the field of play. Ballpark ushers sometimes wrestled the balls away from souvenir-hungry fans. Ed Barrow, the manager of the Boston Red Sox and later the president of the New York Yankees, began the practice of allowing fans to keep balls hit into the stands.

◆

Abner Doubleday came up with a scheme for playing baseball as a real game in his home town of Cooperstown, New York in 1839.

CHAPTER 3
Let's Play Ball

Now let's hear some baseball chatter from the home team. Grab your gloves and hustle out onto the diamond. Get in good ready positions. The pitcher is about to face the first batter.

There's no more time for talk. You know the layout of the diamond and the dimensions of the ballpark. You know the rules of the game and all of the positions. You know the terms, the slang and even how to keep the scorebook.

What? Not all of you know the exact distance between each base, what a 6-4-3 double play is, or what it means if a player has rabbit ears? Read on. You'll find those answers and many other fast, fun facts about all kinds of measurements, rules, terms, slang and much more. So why wait any longer? Let's play ball!

◆

The pitcher's rubber or plate is 24 inches long and 6 inches wide.

◆

The pitcher's rubber is 60 feet, 6 inches from home plate.

◆

A "changeup" is a slow pitch intended to upset a batter's timing.

◆

A "knuckleball" pitch does not spin. It seems to float or wobble to the plate.

◆

The "high cheese" is baseball slang for a high fastball usually just out of the strike zone.

To win the pitching Triple Crown, a hurler must lead the league in wins, strikeouts, and earned run average.

◆

The letter K in a baseball scorebook stands for a strikeout.

◆

A pitcher's pivot foot is the foot which is in contact with the pitcher's plate (rubber) as he delivers the pitch.

In Little League, the pitcher's rubber is 46 feet from home plate.

◆

The bullpen in a baseball park is where relief pitchers warm up and wait to be called into the game. It is usually in an enclosed section in the outfield. At the turn of the century, this area was often decorated with a huge bull advertising Bull Durham tobacco, which is where "bullpen" originates from.

◆

In baseball, a "bean ball" is a pitch thrown at a batter's head (or bean).

◆

Foul tips were first counted as strikes in 1895.

◆

The baseball term "battery" refers to the combination of the pitcher and the catcher.

◆

In a baseball scorebook, "BB" means a base on balls or a walk.

It's Your Call

A major league pitcher throws a ball that bounces on the ground before it reaches home plate. After the ball bounces, the batter swings at the ball and hits it over the fence for a home run. Is it legal? It's your call.

Answer: The hit is legal and it counts. A batter may legally hit a ball even if the pitch first touches the ground before it reaches the plate.

A baseball field is called a diamond because when viewed from above, the bases on a field are arranged in a diamond shape.

"Chatter" is a term for words of encouragement players in the field and on the bench call out during the course of play in a baseball game.

◆

A regulation baseball game lasts nine innings. If a winner is not determined in nine innings, extra innings are played until one team is victorious. Teams must get three outs each to complete an inning.

◆

High school baseball teams play games that last only seven innings.

◆

Little League games last six innings.

◆

Professional baseball teams use only wooden bats. College, high school, amateur, and Little League teams use metal bats.

The distance from base to base on a baseball field is 90 feet.

◆

The distance from base to base in Little League is 60 feet.

◆

In baseball, each position on the field is assigned a number to expedite the process of scoring plays. The pitcher is 1. The catcher is 2. The first baseman is 3. The second baseman is 4. The third baseman is 5. The shortstop is 6. The left fielder is 7. The centerfielder is 8. The right fielder is 9.

◆

A ground ball hit to the shortstop relayed to the second baseman for a force out and then thrown to the first baseman to record an out on the batter would be scored as a 6-4-3 DP (Double Play).

A "triple play" is a rare play by the defense in which three offensive players are legally put out as a result of the continuous action by a fielder or fielders.

◆

An "error" is a fielding mistake on a play that should be made. In the scorebook, it is noted as an E.

◆

The act of throwing a ball from third to second to first is called "around the horn." It originates from the longest possible way to sail from the Atlantic to the Pacific Oceans by going around Cape Horn at the southern tip of Africa.

◆

In baseball, a fielder is any defensive player.

◆

In baseball slang, a player has "rabbit ears" if that player listens to the chatter of opposing players or fans and allows it to affect his concentration and performance on the field.

A "can of corn" is a high fly ball within easy reach of a fielder who will catch it for an out.

◆

A "banjo hit" is a pop fly that safely falls between two fielders. It is also sometimes called a "Texas leaguer," a "blooper," a "squib," a "plunker," or a "flare."

◆

A "money player" in baseball is a player who performs best in crucial situations.

◆

In 1900, the five-sided home plate was introduced for the first time.

◆

A "double steal" is when two runners attempt to advance to the next base both at the same time by stealing.

◆

A "doubleheader" is two back-to-back baseball games.

In baseball, "AB" stands for at-bats.

◆

The batter's box is a rectangle that measures six feet long and four feet wide.

◆

The position or way a batter stands at the plate as he awaits a pitch to hit is known as his "batting stance."

◆

Batting averages were compiled for the first time in 1865.

◆

A player's batting average measures his ability to hit. A batting average is determined by dividing the number of at-bats into the number of hits collected by a player using a decimal point. For example, if a player has 9 hits in 18 at-bats you divide 18 into 9.000, which gives the player a .500 batting average.

To "choke up" on the bat means to grip the bat several inches up from the bottom or nub. Some experts believe choking up gives a hitter better bat control. However, it also slightly decreases the power of a batter's swing.

◆

The batting order is how the players will come to the plate when their team is on offense. It is a sequence determined by hitting ability and not necessarily position. Usually the best hitters bat from one to five in the order.

◆

The donut weight that batters use as they swing a bat in the on deck circle was developed in 1969 by ex-New York Yankee catcher and coach Elston Howard in conjunction with the General Sportscraft Corporation of Bergenfield, New Jersey.

◆

The "cleanup" hitter in a batting order is the player who hits in the No. 4 spot.

"Hitting for the cycle" in baseball means a batter getting a single, double, triple, and home run all in the same game.

It's Your Call

A batter has two strikes. He swings at the next pitch and hits a foul tip. The ball hits the umpire and is then caught by the catcher before it touches the ground. Is the batter out? It's your call.

Answer: No. The ball is dead and the batter cannot be called out.

"On deck" means the player who is waiting to bat next. The "on deck circle" is a special area between the dugout and home plate where that batter awaits his turn to hit.

◆

RBI is short for Run(s) Batted In. RBIs were first added to box scores in 1920.

◆

To win the Triple Crown in baseball, a batter must lead the league in home runs, RBIs, and batting average.

◆

A "dinger" in baseball slang is a home run.

◆

In baseball, a "slump" is a long period of at-bats and games where a batter goes hitless.

Hall of Fame manager Miller Huggins was asked what a hitter in a slump needs most. "A string of good alibis," replied Huggins.

◆

"Speed slows up the game of baseball," said MLB announcer and former big league catcher Tim McCarver. It sounds silly, but it really isn't. What McCarver meant is that a speedy runner on base requires the constant attention of the pitcher. In order to prevent the runner from taking big leads, the pitcher usually makes frequent throws to first base. The throw to first takes extra time and the game usually lasts longer.

◆

In 2004, New York Mets announcer and Baseball Hall of Famer Ralph Kiner repeated this old saying about the art of hitting. Kiner remarked, "It's a round bat and a round ball and you have to hit it squarely."

If a batter is "caught looking," it means that he took a called third strike without swinging at the ball.

◆

Adrian Constantine "Cap" Anson is believed to have invented baseball's hit and run play.

◆

In baseball, a "switch hitter" is a player who can bat both left-handed and right-handed.

◆

In baseball, the third base position is known as the "hot corner."

◆

A "laser" is a sharp, hard-hit line drive in baseball jargon.

◆

If a batted ball hits a base runner while he is off base and in fair territory, that runner is declared out and the ball is dead.

A baseball has a center of cork or hard rubber. Yarn is wrapped around the center. The outside is made of white horsehide stitched together with thick thread. It weighs between five and five and one quarter ounces.

◆

A "bunt" is a special kind of batted ball. A pitch is not swung at. The ball is gently tapped off the bat so it does not go too far from home plate.

◆

Shortstop Richard "Dickey" Pearce is believed to be the first baseball player to utilize the bunt as an offensive weapon. Pearce began using the bunt in 1866.

◆

A "squeeze play" occurs with a runner on third base. A batter at the plate attempts to bring the runner home to score by bunting the ball.

It's Your Call

If a pitcher throws a ball that bounces in front of the batter's box and then skips up and hits the batter, is the hitter awarded first base? It's your call.

Answer: It depends. If the batter makes an attempt to avoid the ball and is hit, the batter is awarded first base. If the batter does not move, but in the umpire's judgment had no chance to avoid the ball, he is also awarded first base. However, if the batter does not move on purpose and tries to be struck by a bounced pitch outside the strike zone, the hitter does not get first base and the pitch is called a ball.

A "sacrifice" is when a batter bunts a ball in an attempt to advance a runner to the next base, putting that runner in a position to score. Usually a sacrifice advances a runner to second as the batter is retired or put out at first base. In this play, the batter sacrifices himself as an out for the good of the team. A successful sacrifice does not count as an at-bat.

◆

A sacrifice fly occurs with a runner on third base. The batter hits a fly ball to the outfield. The runner "tags up" or stays on the base until the ball is caught. The base runner then goes home to score. The batter is credited with an RBI. A sacrifice fly does not count as an at-bat.

◆

In baseball, a two-base hit is known as a "double." A three-base hit is known as a "triple."

The American League uses a "designated hitter rule." A batter who is a good offensive player usually hits for the pitcher. The DH does not play in the field and can actually bat for any weak hitter in the lineup. However, it is almost always the pitcher.

◆

The National League does not use a designated hitter.

◆

A "bat boy" is usually a youngster or teenager who picks up bats after a player takes his turn at bat. The bat boy also handles and organizes bats for players.

◆

A "shoestring" catch is when a fielder bends over very low to snare a ball on the fly just before it touches the ground. The player literally scoops the ball off his shoestrings.

A "circus catch" is a spectacular catch of a fly ball.

◆

A "double play" is a play by the defense in which two offensive players are legally put out as the result of a continuous action.

◆

Sunday baseball games were first played in the National League in 1892.

◆

The first turnstiles were used at baseball stadiums in 1878.

◆

A "farm team" is a minor league baseball club affiliated with a major league team.

◆

A "rhubarb" is a loud argument in baseball usually between a manager or player and an umpire.

CHAPTER 4
Around the Infield

Who's on first? What is the name of the second baseman? Where is the third baseman? If you want me to tell you the name of the shortstop, I don't know. The following tidbits of information, however, will answer your questions and give you a chance to catch up on the exciting exploits of those awesome athletes who play or have played in baseball's infield.

IN THE FIRST PLACE

◆

First baseman Don Mattingly of the New York Yankees won nine Gold Glove Awards for his flawless fielding.

◆

In 1969, Harmon Killebrew of the Minnesota Twins belted 49 home runs and drove in 140 runs to win the American League's Most Valuable Player Award.

◆

Todd Zeile, who played first base for a number of major league teams, including the New York Mets, is a descendant of United States President John Quincy Adams.

◆

First baseman Doug Mientkiewicz hit his first career grand slam on April 21, 2005, while playing for the New York Mets against the Florida Marlins.

Keith Hernandez won 11 consecutive Gold Gloves at first base from 1978 to 1988.

◆

In 1979, first baseman Willie Stargell of the Pittsburgh Pirates was the MVP of the National League Championship Series.

◆

Lou Gehrig of the New York Yankees replaced first baseman Wally Pipp in the Yankee lineup on June 2, 1925 and had three hits in five at bats, eight putouts, and one assist. He also scored a run. Pipp never cracked the Yankee starting lineup again and was later traded. Gehrig went on to play 2,130 games at first base for the Yankees.

◆

Jim Thome hit his 400th career home run while playing first base for the Philadelphia Phillies in a game against the Cincinnati Reds on June 14, 2004.

Sizzler Sizzles on the Plate

First baseman George Sisler of the St. Louis Browns played football, basketball, and baseball at the University of Michigan. As a pro baseball player, Sisler batted .353 in 1917, .341 in 1918, and .352 in 1919. In 1920, George Sisler collected 257 hits and posted a .407 batting average. Sisler hit .371 in 1921 and then banged out 246 hits in 1922 for a hefty .420 batting average. No major league first baseman had ever had six better seasons in a row as a hitter.

In 1967, Orlando Cepeda played first base for the St. Louis Cardinals and won the National League's Most Valuable Player Award. Cepeda batted .325, blasted 25 home runs, and drove in 111 runs that season.

◆

Batter Frank Chance was hit by a pitch five times in one game while playing first base for the Chicago Cubs on May 30, 1904.

◆

Derrek Lee, the Chicago Cubs' first baseman, was the 2005 National League batting champion. Lee had a .335 average that season. He also cracked 46 homers and drove in 107 runs that year.

◆

First sacker Carlos Delgado of the New York Mets slugged the 380th home run of his career against the Pittsburgh Pirates on May 3, 2006.

David Ortiz of the Boston Red Sox is usually his team's designated hitter. When he does play in the field, Ortiz is a first baseman. In 2005, David Ortiz bashed 47 home runs and drove in 148 runs.

◆

Outfielder Frank Howard of the Washington Senators stood six-feet, seven-inches tall and was an All-American in baseball and basketball at Ohio State University. He was drafted by the NBA.

◆

Gil Hodges played mainly first base for the Los Angeles Dodgers in 1959 and blasted 25 homers to lead the Dodgers in home runs that season.

◆

In 2005, first baseman Rafael Palmeiro of the Baltimore Orioles became the first Hispanic player in baseball history to collect 3,000 hits and to smash 500 home runs.

Nickname Game

See if you can correctly match each of the following big league first basemen with his famous nickname:

1. Frank Thomas
   (Chicago White Sox)

2. Bill Skowron
   (New York Yankees)

3. Harmon Killebrew
   (Minnesota Twins)

4. Steve Garvey
   (Los Angeles Dodgers)

5. Dick Stuart
   (Boston Red Sox)

6. Orlando Cepeda
   (St. Louis Cardinals)

A. Moose

B. The Baby Bull

C. Mr. Clean

D. Dr. Strangeglove

E. The Big Hurt

F. Killer

94

Here are the correct answers:

1: E. Frank Thomas of the Chicago White Sox is known as the "Big Hurt." Thomas swings so hard and is such a good power hitter he puts a big hurt on the ball.

2: A. Bill Skowron of the New York Yankees was known as "Moose" because of his burly build.

3: F. Harmon Killebrew of the Minnesota Twins was nicknamed "Killer" because he killed the ball when he hit it.

4: C. Steve Garvey of the Los Angeles Dodgers was called "Mr. Clean" because he was such a clean-cut person and player.

5: D. Dick Stuart of the Boston Red Sox was such a bad fielder his teammates dubbed him "Dr. Strangeglove."

6: B. Orlando Cepeda of the St. Louis Cardinals stood six-feet, two-inches tall and weighed a muscular 210 pounds so he was nicknamed "The Baby Bull."

First baseman Albert Pujols of the St. Louis Cardinals had a .430 on base percentage in 2005. Pujols had 195 hits and 97 walks that season.

◆

Tino Martinez earned four World Series rings playing first base for the New York Yankees from 1996 to 2001.

◆

In 2005, first baseman Mike Jacobs, of the New York Mets, hit a home run in his first major league at-bat.

◆

Willie McCovey joined the San Francisco Giants as a first baseman in July 1959. In his first game, McCovey went four for four at the plate with two triples.

◆

In 1979, Keith Hernandez of the St. Louis Cardinals won the National League batting title with a .344 average.

Chris Chambliss played first base for the Cleveland Indians in 1973.

◆

Felipe Alou played first base for the New York Yankees in 1973.

◆

Joe Torre played first base for the St. Louis Cardinals in 1973.

◆

Joe Lis played first base for the Minnesota Twins in 1973.

◆

Tony Perez played first base for the Cincinnati Reds in 1973.

◆

In 1980, Bill Buckner of the Chicago Cubs won the National League batting title with a .324 average.

First baseman Andres Galarraga retired from baseball in 2005. Galarraga had a career batting average of .288 and blasted 399 home runs.

◆

Jason Giambi was the New York Yankees first baseman in 2005 and 2006.

◆

First baseman Jimmy Foxx of the Philadelphia Athletics was voted the Most Valuable Player of the American League in 1932, 1933, and 1938.

Mark McGwire was the American League Rookie of the Year in 1987 as a first baseman for the Oakland Athletics.

◆

Philadelphia Phillies first baseman Ryan Howard was the National League Rookie of the Year in 2005. Howard batted .288 and had 22 home runs and 63 RBIs in his first big league season.

Rafael Palmeiro, the Baltimore Orioles' first sacker, hit the 563rd home run of his career on June 28, 2005 in a game against the New York Yankees. The blast gave Palmeiro 1,813 career RBIs, making him No. 15 on the all-time career RBI list.

◆

First baseman Albert Pujols is the first player in major league history to hit 30 or more home runs in each of his first four seasons in the big leagues.

In 1986, Will Clark of the San Francisco Giants hit a home run in his first major league at-bat off Houston Astros pitcher Nolan Ryan.

◆

First baseman George Burns of the Boston Red Sox made an unassisted triple play against the Cleveland Indians on September 14, 1923.

First baseman Jeff Bagwell and second baseman Craig Biggio of the Houston Astros are known as the "Killer Bs."

◆

Marvelous Marv Throneberry, who played first base for the New York Mets in 1962, was a notoriously poor fielder. On Throneberry's birthday, his Met teammate, Richie Ashburn, walked over and shook his hand. "Happy Birthday, Marv," said Ashburn, "we were going to give you a cake, but we thought you'd drop it."

◆

Todd Helton of the Colorado Rockies batted .358 in 2003. He finished second to Albert Pujols of the St. Louis Cardinals in the race for the National League batting crown. Pujols won the title that season with a .359 average.

First Last Words

Major league first baseman Al Oliver once said, "There's no such thing as bragging. You're either lying or telling the truth."

While he was playing first base for the Philadelphia Phillies, Pete Rose was asked about his pro baseball career. "With the money I'm making, I should be playing two positions," said Rose.

◆

First baseman Steve Garvey of the Los Angeles Dodgers was asked about his priorities as a player. Said Garvey, "It's more important to have fun than to be great."

NO SECOND GUESSING

◆

Arizona Diamondback second baseman Craig Counsell was the MVP of the National League Championship Series in 2001.

◆

Toni Stone was the first African-American woman to play professional baseball. Stone played second base for the Indianapolis Clowns of the Old Negro League in 1953 and batted .243 in her rookie season.

◆

Second baseman Luis Castillo of the Florida Marlins stole 48 bases in 2002 to lead the National League.

◆

Julio Franco of the Texas Rangers was voted the Most Valuable Player of the 1990 All-Star game for his outstanding play at second base.

Rogers Hornsby won the National League batting championship seven times while playing second base for the St. Louis Cardinals. Hornsby, who was nicknamed "The Rajah," had a lifetime batting average of .358. In 1924, the Rajah batted an incredible .424!

◆

In 2002, second baseman Adam Kennedy of the Anaheim Angels was the Most Valuable Player of the American League Championship Series.

◆

Pete Rose of the Cincinnati Reds was a second baseman when he was named the National League Rookie of the Year in 1963.

◆

Micky Morandini pulled off an unassisted triple play against the Pittsburgh Pirates while playing second base for the Philadelphia Phillies on September 20, 1992.

Bobby Richardson played second base for the New York Yankees in 1959 and batted .301.

◆

Ryne Sandberg won nine Gold Gloves as a second baseman from 1983 to 1991.

◆

Chicago White Sox second baseman Nellie Fox was voted the Most Valuable Player of the American League in 1959. Fox posted a .306 batting average that season.

◆

Joe Morgan of the Cincinnati Reds won five Gold Gloves as a second baseman from 1973 to 1977.

◆

In 2002, Alfonso Soriano batted .300, smacked 39 home runs, and collected 102 RBIs while playing second base for the New York Yankees.

All-Star second baseman Bret Boone hit over 250 home runs during his major league career.

◆

Second baseman Ryne Sandberg was elected to the Baseball Hall of Fame in 2005. During his career, Sandberg appeared in 2,164 games and pounded out 2,386 hits, for a .285 career batting average. He also clouted 282 home runs, scored 1,318 runs, and stole 344 bases.

◆

Rod Carew of the Minnesota Twins was named the American League Rookie of the Year in 1967 as a second baseman. In 1977, Carew was voted the Most Valuable Player in the American League as a first baseman.

A First-Rate Play at Second Base

Baseball history was made on October 10, 1920 when the Cleveland Indians played the Brooklyn Dodgers in the fifth game of the World Series. Playing second base for Cleveland was William Wambsganss. In the top of the fifth, the Dodgers had runners Pete Kilduff on second and Otto Miller on first with no outs. Clarence Mitchell of Brooklyn was at the plate. Mitchell swung and crushed a screaming line drive up the middle. William Wambsganss reacted instinctively and managed to snare the ball for out number one. Kilduff was caught off second base. Wambsganss then raced to second and tagged the base for out number two. But the play wasn't over yet. Otto Miller was frozen between first and second base. Wambsganss ran down Miller and tagged him for out number three! On that day, William Wambsganss pulled off the first unassisted triple play in World Series history.

Sparky Anderson, who later became a successful big league manager, played second base for the Philadelphia Phillies in 1959. Anderson was a better manager than a hitter. His batting average in 1959 was a mere .218.

New York Yankees second baseman Joe Gordon had the strange habit of changing bats every time he went up to hit. Just for luck, Gordon never used the same bat in two consecutive at bats.

Young second baseman Bill Mazeroski of the Pittsburgh Pirates was known as a slick fielder who wasn't much of a hitter when he first came into the big leagues. At a press conference a Pirates official told newsmen, "Bill Mazeroski is a clean-cut, church-going youngster who is a model for teenagers." A reporter quickly remarked, "That may be so, but the Pirates might be better off with a juvenile delinquent who can hit."

On June 29, 2005, second baseman Craig Biggio of the Houston Astros set a major league post-1900 record when he was hit by a pitch for the 268th time in his career. Biggio was plunked by Colorado Rockies pitcher Byung-Hyun Kim.

Second sacker Marcus Giles of the Atlanta Braves is five-feet, eight-inches tall.

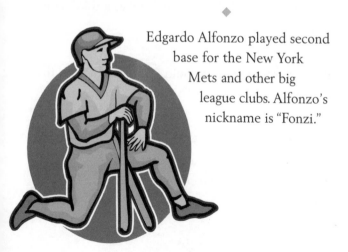

Edgardo Alfonzo played second base for the New York Mets and other big league clubs. Alfonzo's nickname is "Fonzi."

THREE IS NOT A CROWD

♦

Third baseman David Wright was the first New York Mets player to drive in runs in each of the first six games of a season. He did it in 2006.

♦

Chris Sabo of the Cincinnati Reds was the National League Rookie of the Year in 1988 as a third baseman.

♦

Robin Ventura won six Gold Gloves at third in the 1990s.

♦

Third baseman David Bell has baseball in his blood. His father, Buddy Bell, and his grandfather, Gus Bell, both played Major League Baseball.

Third baseman Scott Rolen was the National League's Rookie of the Year in 1997 as a member of the Philadelphia Phillies.

◆

Playing third base for the Milwaukee Brewers on October 12, 1982, Paul Molitor banged out five hits in a 10 to 0 rout of the St. Louis Cardinals in the opening game of the World Series.

◆

Eddie Mathews played third base for the Milwaukee Braves in 1953 and blasted 47 round-trippers. Matthews smashed 512 homers in his career and pounded out 2,315 total hits.

◆

Third baseman Wade Boggs was voted into baseball's Hall of Fame in 2005. Boggs played in 2,439 games and posted a career .328 batting average.

The Vacuum Man

Hall of Fame third baseman Brooks Robinson of the Baltimore Orioles was known as "Hoover" because he vacuumed up ground balls. Robinson made 15 consecutive All-Star appearances starting in 1960. In 1964, Robinson was the MVP of the American League. That season Robinson batted .317, clouted 28 home runs, and collected 118 RBIs. To top things off, Robinson won 16 Gold Glove awards.

Morgan Ensberg was the third baseman for the Houston Astros in 2006. Ensberg batted .283, hit 36 home runs, and drove in 101 runs for the Astros during the 2005 season.

Cletis "Clete" Boyer played third base for the Kansas City Royals and the New York Yankees in the 1950s and 1960s. Clete was also known by his nickname "Spike."

◆

Ken Boyer played third base for the St. Louis Cardinals in the 1950s and 1960s, and was the brother of Clete Boyer. Ken Boyer hit .309 and blasted 28 home runs in 1959.

◆

Third baseman Ron Cey of the Los Angeles Dodgers was nicknamed "Penguin" because his teammates thought he waddled when he walked. Cey shared the Most Valuable Player award of the 1981 World Series with Dodgers teammates Pedro Guerrero and Steve Yeager.

Alex Rodriguez was the American League's Most Valuable Player as a shortstop in 2003. Rodriguez moved to third base when he went from the Texas Rangers to the New York Yankees in 2004. In 2005, A-Rod was named the American League's Most Valuable Player as a third baseman.

◆

In 1999, third baseman Chipper Jones of the Atlanta Braves hit 45 home runs, drove in 110 runs, and posted a .319 batting average to earn the National League's Most Valuable Player award.

◆

Mike Schmidt went to Ohio University and earned a Bachelor's Degree in business administration.

◆

Third baseman Mike Schmidt of the Philadelphia Phillies won back-to-back National League MVP awards in 1980 and 1981. Schmidt crashed 48 home runs and batted .286 in 1980. The following year he belted 31 homers and hit .316.

Buck Weaver, who played third base for the Chicago White Sox in the early 1900s, once hit 17 fouls in a row during an at-bat against the Boston Red Sox. The Boston pitcher Weaver faced was Babe Ruth.

◆

Third baseman Bobby Brown quit pro baseball to become a doctor. After Brown left baseball, his old teammate Gene Woodling joked, "Bobby Brown had such lousy hands when he played third I wouldn't let him operate on me!"

Three on a Match Quiz

Match the following American League Most Valuable Players with the correct team each one played for and the position each one played when he won the award:

Boog Powell
(1970 MVP)

Zoilo Versalles
(1965 MVP)

Al Rosen
(1953 MVP)

Charlie Gehringer
(1937 MVP)

Spud Chandler
(1943 MVP)

1. Cleveland Indians

2. Baltimore Orioles

3. New York Yankees

4. Minnesota Twins

5. Detroit Tigers

A. Pitcher

B. First Base

C. Second Base

D. Third Base

E. Shortstop

Answers

Boog Powell (1970 MVP): 2–B. Powell played for the Baltimore Orioles and was a first baseman.

Zoilo Versalles (1965 MVP): 4–E. Versalles played for the Minnesota Twins and was a shortstop.

Al Rosen (1953 MVP): 1–D. Rosen played for the Cleveland Indians and was a third baseman.

Charlie Gehringer (1937 MVP): 5–C. Gehringer played for the Detroit Tigers and was a second baseman.

Spud Chandler (1943 MVP): 3–A. Chandler played for the New York Yankees and was a pitcher.

COMING UP SHORTSTOP

◆

Ernie Banks batted .304 and smashed 45 home runs while playing shortstop for the Chicago Cubs in 1959.

◆

Hall of Fame centerfielder Mickey Mantle was a shortstop when he joined the New York Yankees as a rookie player in 1951.

◆

Shortstop Ozzie Smith of the St. Louis Cardinals won 13 Gold Glove awards from 1980 to 1992.

◆

Shortstop John Valentin of the Boston Red Sox made an unassisted triple play against the Seattle Mariners on July 8, 1994.

Baltimore Orioles shortstop Cal Ripken, Jr. batted .318, hit 27 home runs, and drove in 102 runs in 1983 to become the Most Valuable Player of the American League.

♦

Oakland Athletics shortstop Bobby Crosby was the 2004 Rookie of the Year in the American League.

♦

David Eckstein is one of the shortest players in the Major Leagues. Eckstein stands five-feet, seven-inches tall. He played shortstop for the St. Louis Cardinals in 2006.

♦

Shortstop John Peter "Honus" Wagner of the Pittsburgh Pirates played in the major leagues for 21 years and appeared in 2,792 games. Wagner had 7,930 put outs and 6,781 assists. He also collected 3,415 hits in his career for a lifetime batting average of .327!

Shortstop Derek Jeter was named the 11th captain of the New York Yankees in June 2003. Jeter collected his 2,000th career hit in a game against the Kansas City Royals on May 26, 2006.

◆

Shortstop Jose Reyes of the New York Mets hit for the cycle (single, double, triple, home run) on June 21, 2006, against the Cincinnati Reds.

◆

Hall of Famer Lou Gehrig played in the first of his 2,130 games on June 1, 1925, when he pinch-hit for New York Yankees shortstop Pee-Wee Wanninger in a game against the Washington Senators.

◆

Shortstop Maury Wills of the Los Angeles Dodgers stole 104 bases in 1962.

Shortstop Miguel Tejada of the Baltimore Orioles was named the Most Valuable Player of the 2005 All-Star game. Tejada hit a home run, drove in another run, and turned a double play to lead the AL over the NL 7 to 5.

◆

Cleveland Indians shortstop Ray Chapman was struck in the head by a pitch thrown by New York Yankees hurler Carl Mays on August 16, 1920, and died in a hospital 12 hours later. Chapman is the only major leaguer to have died from being hit by a pitch.

◆

Dave Concepcion of the Cincinnati Reds was the starting National League shortstop in the 1982 All-Star game and was named the contest's Most Valuable Player.

◆

The Most Valuable Player of the 1978 World Series was shortstop Bucky Dent of the New York Yankees.

Harold "Pee Wee" Reese played shortstop for the Brooklyn Dodgers from 1940 to 1958. Reese played in 2,166 games and pounded out 2,170 hits during his career. He was inducted into the Hall of Fame in 1984.

♦

Shortstop Phil Rizzuto of the New York Yankees was nicknamed "Scooter" because he used to "scoot" after ground balls. In 1950, Rizzuto was voted the MVP of the American League.

♦

Shortstop Jimmy Rollins of the Philadelphia Phillies was added to the 2005 National League All-Star team as a replacement for injured Los Angeles Dodgers shortstop Cesar Izturis.

♦

Old-time shortstop Johnny Logan once explained why his inexperienced team wasn't winning by saying, "Rome wasn't born in a day."

Los Angeles shortstop Maury Wills had this to say while leading his Dodgers teammates in exercises: "Okay, everyone, now inhale, and dehale."

◆

Shortstop Garry Templeton of the St. Louis Cardinals was elected to the 1980 All-Star game as a backup player, but declined to attend the contest. Templeton explained his refusal by saying, "If I ain't startin' . . . I ain't departin'!"

UTILITY WORK AHEAD

◆

Joe McEwing was a utility man for the Kansas City Royals in 2006. McEwing could fill in at any infield or outfield position, and in an emergency could even play catcher.

◆

Ty Wigginton had an interesting role as a utility man for the Tampa Bay Devil Rays in 2006. Wigginton played third base, second base, first base, left field, and right field. However, Wigginton wasn't a substitute off the bench. He hit so well, he started most games, and batted fourth or fifth in the line-up. He just played a variety of defensive positions.

◆

New York Yankees utility player Miguel Cairo filled in at shortstop, third base, second base, and first base in 2006.

CHAPTER 5
In the Outfield

Here's the delivery from the pitcher. It's a high, fast ball. The batter swings. Crack! It's a fly ball in the gap between centerfield and right field. Both outfielders are in hot pursuit of the sizzling horsehide. However, the centerfielder has a great jump on the ball and the only chance of hauling it in. The right fielder, who is better known for his hitting than his fielding, stops short when he hears his teammate yell, "I've got it!"

At a dead run, the centerfielder stretches out his glove and plucks the big fly out of the sky. The batter is out. Another great play has been made by a major league outfielder and an appreciative crowd roars its approval of his circus catch.

Centerfielder Andruw Jones of the Atlanta Braves hit .263, knocked 51 home runs, and collected 128 RBIs during the 2005 season.

◆

In 2004, outfielder Ichiro Suzuki of the Seattle Mariners set a new major league record for hits in a season. Suzuki broke George Sisler's 84-year-old mark by getting an infield single off pitcher Ryan Drese of the Texas Rangers. The hit was Ichiro's 258th of the season. He went 3-for-5 in the game.

◆

Johnny Damon's first home run as a New York Yankees outfielder came on April 13, 2006, in a game against the Kansas City Royals. The Yankees won 9 to 3.

◆

Outfielder Frank Robinson was the first player to win the Most Valuable Player award in both the National League and the American League. In

1961, Robinson was the NL's Most Valuable Player as a member of the Cincinnati Reds. In 1966, he was the AL's Most Valuable Player as a member of the Baltimore Orioles.

◆

Babe Ruth played right field for the New York Yankees and swatted 714 home runs during his major league career.

◆

Roberto Clemente of the Pittsburgh Pirates won 12 Gold Glove awards in the outfield from 1961 to 1972.

◆

Leftfielder Manny Ramirez of the Boston Red Sox won the American League batting crown in 2002. Ramirez hit .349 that season.

◆

Atlanta Braves outfielder Hank Aaron hit his 715th home run on April 8, 1974, off pitcher Al Downing of the Los Angeles Dodgers.

Former St. Louis Cardinals pitcher Rick Ankiel tried to switch to the outfield in 2005. Unfortunately, Ankiel's switch of positions didn't work out and the Cardinals placed him on an unconditional release waiver.

◆

Carl Crawford led the Tampa Bay Devil Rays with 55 stolen bases in 2003.

◆

Right fielder Roberto Clemente won the batting title of the National League in 1964 with a .339 batting average.

◆

Left fielder Hideki Matsui of the New York Yankees is nicknamed "Godzilla" because of his monstrous hitting ability.

◆

Jim Edmonds played centerfield for the St. Louis Cardinals in 2006.

Say, Hey, Willie Mays

Willie Mays was nicknamed the "Say, Hey Kid." He wore No. 24.

Willie Mays spent most of his Major League Baseball career playing centerfield for the New York and San Francisco Giants.

Willie Mays batted .345 playing for the New York Giants in 1954 and hit .347 for the San Francisco Giants in 1958.

Centerfielder Willie Mays of the New York Giants made one of the most famous catches in baseball history in the first game of the 1954

World Series against the Cleveland Indians. With the game tied 2 to 2 in the eighth inning, the Indians had runners on first and second with no outs. Cleveland batter Vic Wertz smashed a deep line drive over Mays' head. The Giants' outfielder raced back without looking and made an amazing over the shoulder catch for the out. Mays then whirled and threw the ball in which kept the Cleveland runners from advancing. The Giants went on to win that game and the World Series.

Coco Crisp played centerfield for the Boston Red Sox in 2006.

◆

Mel Ott played outfield for the New York Giants and belted 511 home runs during his career.

Centerfielder Duke Snider of the Brooklyn Dodgers won the National League's home run title in 1956 by smashing 43 round-trippers.

◆

Sammy Sosa slugged his first home run for the Baltimore Orioles against the Tampa Bay Devil Rays, on April 12, 2005.

◆

Ken Griffey Jr. of the Seattle Mariners led the American League in RBIs in 1997. Griffey had 147 RBIs that season.

Carlos Beltran played for the Kansas City Royals in 2003 and led the team that season with a .307 batting average.

◆

Outfielder Tony Gwynn of the San Diego Padres won five Gold Gloves and collected 3,141 hits during his 20-year major league career.

◆

Carl Yastrzemski of the Boston Red Sox won the American League batting title with a .301 average in 1968.

◆

Paul O'Neill of the New York Yankees won the American League batting title in 1994 with a .359 batting average.

◆

Philadelphia Phillies outfielder Bobby Abreau won the All-Star home run derby contest in 2005 by smacking a total of 41 dingers.

Family Ties

On September 15, 1963, all three Alou brothers—Felipe, Matty, and Jesus—played in the outfield for the San Francisco Giants in a 13 to 5 win over the Pittsburgh Pirates.

Moises Alou played outfield for the San Francisco Giants in 2006. The manager of San Francisco that year was Felipe Alou, the father of Moises Alou.

Outfielder Matty Alou of the Pittsburgh Pirates hit .342 in 1966 to capture the batting title of the National League.

Outfielder Miguel Cabrera of the Florida Marlins was a reserve for the National League All-Stars in 2005.

◆

Luis Gonzalez of the Arizona Diamondbacks collected 206 hits in 1999 to lead the National League.

◆

Larry Walker of the Colorado Rockies smashed 49 dingers in 1997 to win the home run crown of the National League.

◆

Richard Hidalgo of the Houston Astros hit .309 in 2003.

◆

Willie Davis of the Los Angeles Dodgers hit safely in 31 consecutive games in 1969.

Hall of Fame outfielder Joe Medwick, who played for the St. Louis Cardinals in the 1930s, was nicknamed "Ducky."

◆

Lewis "Hack" Wilson of the Chicago Cubs hit 56 home runs in 1930.

◆

Outfielder Sadaharu Oh of Tokyo's Yomiuri Giants hit 868 home runs during his 22-year career.

◆

Outfielder Harry Heilmann of the Detroit Tigers won American League batting titles in 1921 (.394 average), 1923 (.403 average), 1925 (.393 average), and in 1927 (.398 average). Heilmann later became a radio announcer for Detroit Tigers games.

◆

New York Yankees outfielder Mickey Mantle collected 2,415 hits during his 18-year major league career.

A centerfielder is the captain of the outfield. A centerfielder takes all balls he can reach in the gaps between left and right fields.

◆

Ted Williams of the Boston Red Sox won the American League batting crown in 1957 for the fifth time by posting a .388 average.

◆

Roberto Clemente of the Pittsburgh Pirates collected exactly 3,000 hits during his major league career. The star outfielder would have added to his total if he had not perished in a plane crash while doing charity work on New Year's Eve 1972.

◆

Vladimir Guerrero of the Montreal Expos hit 34 home runs and stole 37 bases during the 2001 season.

Ralph Kiner blasted a career-high 54 home runs for the Pittsburgh Pirates in 1949. He led the National League in homers from 1946 to 1952.

◆

Outfielder Dave Winfield of the University of Minnesota went straight to the major leagues after being drafted by the San Diego Padres in 1973.

◆

Roger Maris played for the Cleveland Indians, Kansas City Athletics, New York Yankees, and the St. Louis Cardinals. As a member of the New York Yankees in 1961, Maris set the major league record by blasting 61 home runs.

◆

In Roger Maris' first game as an outfielder for the 1960 New York Yankees, he smashed two home runs, a double, and a single.

Roger Maris was voted the Most Valuable Player in the American League in 1960. Maris clubbed 39 homers that year. Teammate Mickey Mantle finished second in the voting.

◆

In 1951, Mickey Mantle was called up from the minors to the New York Yankees as a replacement for centerfielder Joe DiMaggio, who was injured.

◆

Paul and Lloyd Waner played outfield for the Pittsburgh Pirates from the late 1920s to the 1940s. Paul was nicknamed "Big Poison" because he was the bigger brother. Lloyd was named "Little Poison." The Waner Brothers were lethal hitters. In 1927, Lloyd Waner collected 223 hits as a rookie. Paul Waner collected 3,152 hits in his 20-year career. Both were elected to the Hall of Fame.

◆

Sammy Sosa of the Chicago Cubs stole 36 bases and blasted 33 home runs in 1993.

Left fielder George Foster of the Cincinnati Reds was named the Most Valuable Player of the National League in 1977. Foster hit 52 homers, batted .320, collected 149 RBI's, and scored 124 runs that year.

◆

A right fielder usually has the best throwing arm of a team's three outfielders.

◆

Outfielder Ty Cobb of the Detroit Tigers won his first American League batting title in 1907 with a .350 average.

◆

Lou Brock stole 118 bases in 153 games in 1974 as an outfielder for the St. Louis Cardinals.

◆

Outfielder Ty Cobb of the Detroit Tigers stole 96 bases in 1915, and led the American League.

Tris Speaker was a star centerfielder for the Boston Red Sox in the early 1900s and is a member of Baseball's Hall of Fame. In 1916, he led the American League in hitting with a .386 average while playing for the Cleveland Indians. Speaker collected 11 hits in a row on July 8, 9, and 10 in 1920. He also clubbed 793 doubles during his career.

◆

Casey Stengel, who is considered to be one of baseball's most colorful managers, was an outfielder during his major league playing days. Stengel played outfield for the Brooklyn Dodgers, the Milwaukee Braves, the Philadelphia Phillies, and the New York Giants. He had a .284 lifetime batting average.

◆

Jose Conseco of the Oakland Athletics smashed 42 homers and stole 40 bases during the 1988 major league season.

Pete Gray, who played outfield for the St. Louis Browns of the American League in 1945, had only one arm. Gray was a respectable fielder and a decent hitter.

◆

In 1941, the New York Yankees outfield was made up of left fielder Charley Keller, centerfielder Joe DiMaggio, and right fielder Tommy Henrich.

◆

Star outfielders Reggie Jackson and Carl Yastrzemski both played Little League baseball.

◆

Outfielder Rocky Colavito of the Cleveland Indians hit four consecutive home runs on June 10, 1959.

◆

Outfielder Reggie Jackson was nicknamed "Mr. October" because of his uncanny ability to perform amazing feats in the World Series and playoffs.

Stan Musial of the St. Louis Cardinals hit .346 in 1950 to capture the National League batting title.

◆

Carlos Lee of the Milwaukee Brewers was a reserve outfielder on the National League All-Star team in 2005.

◆

Outfielder Bernie Williams of the New York Yankees collected the 2,000th hit of his major league career on June 10, 2004, in an interleague game against the Colorado Rockies.

◆

Outfielder Ron LeFore was a model prisoner on the Michigan State Prison baseball team when he was noticed by big league manager Billy Martin of the Detroit Tigers. When LeFore was released in the early 1970s, Martin gave him a tryout. LeFore ended up making the Tigers squad as a centerfielder.

Cincinnati Reds outfielder Ken Griffey, Jr. blasted the 548th home run of his career against the New York Mets on June 19, 2006. Griffey homered off Orlando Hernandez to tie Mike Schmidt for 12th place on the all-time list.

◆

Tony Oliva of the Minnesota Twins had the top batting average in the American League in 1964, with .323.

◆

Gary Sheffield of the San Diego Padres won the National League batting title with a .330 average in 1992.

◆

Manny Ramirez of the Boston Red Sox hit the 400th home run of his career on May 15, 2005. Ramirez's fence-clearing clout came against pitcher Gil Meche of the Seattle Mariners.

Lenny Dykstra collected 192 hits in 1990. He shared the National League title in that category that season with Brett Butler of the San Francisco Giants.

◆

In 1998, Kirby Puckett of the Minnesota Twins led the American League with 234 hits.

◆

Lance Berkman of the Houston Astros scored 110 runs in 2003.

◆

Tony Conigliaro was 19 years old when he started in the outfield for the Boston Red Sox. In his first game, he played against the New York Yankees and singled off Hall of Famer Whitey Ford.

◆

Garrett Anderson of the Anaheim Angels hit .315 in 2003 and drove in 116 runs.

In 1992, Barry Bonds of the Pittsburgh Pirates led the National League with 109 runs scored.

◆

Tommie Agee of the New York Mets hit for the cycle (single, double, triple, homer) against the St. Louis Cardinals on July 6, 1970.

◆

Vladimir Guerrero of the Montreal Expos hit safely in 31 consecutive games in 1999.

◆

Dave Kingman of the Chicago Cubs won the home run title of the National League in 1979 by belting 48.

◆

Richie Ashburn played in 730 consecutive games.

◆

Jeff Bagwell of the Houston Astros scored 143 runs in 1999 to lead the National League.

Ty Cobb once said, "Every great batter works on the theory that the pitcher is more afraid of him than he is of the pitcher."

Rule Reversal

Jimmy Piersall was a talented but zany outfielder who played for the Boston Red Sox and the New York Mets. Piersall was a member of the Mets when he hit the 100th home run of his major league career. To celebrate his achievement, he came up with a novel twist. He circled the bases while running backwards. The fans enjoyed Piersall's wacky stunt, but baseball rule makers did not. The following year they passed a rule outlawing backward base-running after a home run.

CHAPTER 6
Here's the Pitch!

Rapid Robert Feller! Nolan Ryan! Lefty Grove! Pedro Martinez! Grover Cleveland Alexander! Tom Seaver! Bob Gibson! Vida Blue! Randy Johnson! Cy Young! Sandy Koufax! Warren Spahn! These are just a few pitchers in a long, illustrious list of baseball's best pitchers. It begins way back with hurlers like Happy Jack Chesbro and fast-forwards to current diamond stars like Dontrelle Willis. These are the athletes who know all the ins and outs of home plate. They are hot stuff when it comes to heaters. They know how to bend the rules when it comes to breaking pitches. They throw cutters, sinkers, and enjoy an occasional change of pace. Last but not least, when it comes to the alphabet, without a doubt their favorite letter is K!

Relief pitcher Dennis Eckersley was voted into Baseball's Hall of Fame in 2004. He was the first pitcher who worked mainly as a one-inning closer to be enshrined in the Hall.

◆

Pedro Martinez of the New York Mets recorded the 200th pitching victory of his career on April 17, 2006. Martinez's milestone win came in a 4 to 3 victory over the Atlanta Braves.

◆

Mickey Lolich of the Detroit Tigers won three complete games while pitching against the St. Louis Cardinals in the 1968 World Series.

Roger Clemens recorded the 300th win and the 4,000th strikeout of his career pitching for the New York Yankees in a 5 to 2 victory over the St. Louis Cardinals. Oddly enough, Clemens' good luck game came on Friday the 13th in June 2004.

◆

Pitcher Mike O'Connor of the Washington Nationals got his first major league win by beating the New York Mets 6 to 2 on May 2, 2006.

◆

Rick Mahler made four consecutive opening day starts on the pitching mound for the Atlanta Braves beginning in 1985.

◆

In 2006, pitcher Bruce Sutter of the Chicago Cubs was elected to the Baseball Hall of Fame. Sutter was one of the first relief specialists to be elected to the Hall. Sutter helped revolutionize the split-fingered fastball and was a Cy Young winner in 1979. He recorded 300 saves in 12 major league seasons.

Pitcher Jim Kaat won 16 Gold Glove awards.

◆

Mariano Rivera of the New York Yankees recorded the 300th save of his career on May 28, 2004 against the Tampa Bay Devil Rays. Rivera picked up his historic save in a 7 to 5 Yankees victory.

◆

On September 26, 1981, Nolan Ryan of the Houston Astros pitched the fifth no-hitter of his career. It was a 5 to 0 victory over the Los Angeles Dodgers at the Houston Astrodome.

◆

Kenny Rogers of the Detroit Tigers won the 200th game of his pitching career by beating the Chicago Cubs 12 to 3 in an interleague game on June 18, 2006.

Bartolo Colon of the Anaheim Angels was the only 20-game winner in the American League in 2005. Colon had a season record of 21 wins and 8 losses and an ERA of 3.48. He also struck out 157 batters in 222.2 innings. For his work on the mound in 2005, Colon was named the winner of the American League's Cy Young Award.

◆

Greg Maddux of the Chicago Cubs earned the 300th victory of his career pitching against the San Francisco Giants on August 7, 2004. The Cubs beat the Giants 8 to 4.

◆

Bobby Shantz won eight Gold Gloves for his fielding as a pitcher.

◆

Former major league pitcher Sparky Lyle was the manager of the Somerset Patriots, an independent minor league team in New Jersey, in 2006.

Walter Johnson of the Washington Senators earned the 300th win of his career on May 14, 1920, by beating the Detroit Tigers 9 to 8.

◆

Dodgers closer Eric Gagne recorded his 80th save in a row on June 18, 2004, when Los Angeles beat the New York Yankees.

◆

Pitcher Jim Abbott of Michigan won the Golden Spikes Award in 1987 as America's best amateur player.

◆

Fred Toney of the Cincinnati Reds and Hippo Vaughn of the Chicago Cubs pitched a double no-hitter over nine innings on May 2, 1917. The Reds won the game in the 10th inning as multi-sport superstar Jim Thorpe drove in the winning run for a 1 to 0 victory.

Pitcher Dontrelle Willis of the Florida Marlins was named to the All-Star team in 2003 just two months after he was called up to the big leagues from the minors.

◆

Dontrelle Willis played Little League baseball in Alameda, California.

◆

On August 8, 1920, it took pitcher Howard Ehmke of the Detroit Tigers only one hour and thirteen minutes to defeat the New York Yankees 1 to 0. It was one of the fastest major league pitching victories on record.

◆

Nolan Ryan of the California Angels struck out 19 Boston Red Sox batters in a 4 to 2 win on August 12, 1974.

Babe Ruth pitched against Walter Johnson on May 7, 1917. Ruth's Boston Red Sox defeated Johnson's Washington Senators 1 to 0. Babe gave up only two hits and drove in the winning run by hitting a sacrifice fly!

◆

Pitcher Lew Burdette of the Milwaukee Braves pitched and won three complete games against the New York Yankees in the 1957 World Series.

◆

David Cone of the New York Yankees pitched a perfect game against the Montreal Expos on July 18, 1999.

◆

Pitcher Cy Young of the Cleveland Indians won the 500th game of his career on May 19, 1910, when he beat the Washington Senators 5 to 4 in 11 innings.

St. Louis Cardinals pitcher Bob Gibson won 9 Gold Glove awards.

◆

Pitcher Johan Santana of the Minnesota Twins was the American League's Cy Young Award winner in 2004.

◆

Relief pitcher John Franco served as the captain of the New York Mets during the 2004 season.

◆

Grover Cleveland Alexander of the Philadelphia Phillies pitched four one-hitters in 1915.

◆

Pitcher Robert Shaw of the Milwaukee Braves recorded eight balks during the 1963 season.

◆

Jerry Koosman pitched in the big leagues for 19 seasons and struck out 2,556 batters.

Don't Strike Out

Match the following pitchers with the correct year each one was named the Most Valuable Player in the American League and the team each one played for when he won the award.

Vida Blue   1. 1945   A. Milwaukee Brewers

Hal Newhouser 2. 1971   B. Oakland A's

Rollie Fingers 3. 1981   C. Detroit Tigers

Answers: The correct matches are: Vida Blue, 2–B; Hal Newhouser, 1–C; and Rollie Fingers: 3–A.

David Wells recorded his 200th career victory on September 28, 2003, while pitching the New York Yankees to a 3 to 1 victory over the Baltimore Orioles.

◆

Randy Johnson of the Arizona Diamondbacks pitched a perfect game against the Atlanta Braves on May 18, 2004. Arizona beat Atlanta 2 to 0. Johnson's pitching gem was the 17th perfect game in major league history.

◆

Ron Guidry of the New York Yankees struck out 18 California Angels in one game on June 17, 1978.

◆

Len Barker of the Cleveland Indians pitched a perfect game against the Toronto Blue Jays on May 15, 1981. The Indians beat the Jays 3 to 0.

Hideo Nomo of the Boston Red Sox pitched a no-hitter against the Baltimore Orioles on April 4, 2001.

◆

Pitcher Mark Prior of USC won the Golden Spikes Award in 2001 as America's best amateur player.

◆

Steve Carlton struck out 4,136 batters during his 24-year pitching career.

◆

On August 7, 1956, 50-year-old Satchel Paige pitched in a minor league game in the International League and won the contest.

◆

Pitcher John Ryan had 10 wild pitches in a single National League game in 1876.

◆

Bert Blyleven pitched in the major leagues for 22 years and struck out 3,701 batters.

Christy Mathewson of the New York Giants had four World Series shutout victories from 1905 to 1913.

◆

Tug McGraw was a relief pitcher for the New York Mets and the Philadelphia Phillies. He is also the father of country western music star Tim McGraw.

◆

Randy Johnson recorded the 4,400th strikeout of his career while pitching for the New York Yankees against the Tampa Bay Devil Rays on May 4, 2006. The batter Johnson fanned to notch his milestone was Nick Green.

◆

Walter Johnson of the Washington Senators had four wild pitches in a single inning in a game played on September 21, 1914.

Ed Reulbach of the Chicago Cubs pitched a one-hitter against the Chicago White Sox in the World Series on October 10, 1906.

♦

Kevin Millwood of the Philadelphia Phillies hurled a no-hitter on April 27, 2003 as he beat the San Francisco Giants 1 to 0.

♦

Pitcher Don Sutton of the Milwaukee Brewers recorded the 3,000th strikeout of his career on June 24, 1983. Sutton's 3,000th victim at the plate was batter Alan Bannister of the Cleveland Indians.

♦

Ferguson Jenkins struck out 3,192 batters during his 19-year career as a big league pitcher.

♦

Barry Zito of the Oakland Athletics recorded the 1,000th strikeout of his pitching career on June 1, 2006 against the Minnesota Twins. The contest was also Zito's 200th career start as a pitcher.

Tom Glavine of the Atlanta Braves won the National League Cy Young Award in 1998 when he posted a record of 20 wins and 6 losses.

◆

Ed Reulbach of the Chicago Cubs pitched both games of a doubleheader on September 26, 1908, and recorded back-to-back shutouts. Reulbach blanked the Brooklyn Dodgers 5 to 0 in game one and shut out the Dodgers 3 to 0 in game two.

◆

Pitcher Kris Benson of the Baltimore Orioles hit the first home run of his major league career while pitching the Orioles to a 4 to 2 victory over the New York Mets on June 17, 2006.

◆

Don Sutton won his 300th game on June 18, 1986, when he pitched the California Angels to a 5 to 1 triumph over the Texas Rangers.

Pitcher Steve Carlton of the St. Louis Cardinals struck out 19 New York Mets in a nine-inning game on September 15, 1969, and still lost the contest 4 to 3. New York's Ron Swoboda clouted two two-run homers.

◆

George Wiltse of the New York Giants pitched a 10-inning no-hitter against the Philadelphia Phillies on July 4, 1908 and won 1 to 0.

◆

Bob Forsch of the St. Louis Cardinals threw a no-hitter against the Philadelphia Phillies, beating them 5 to 0 on April 16, 1978. Ken Forsch of the Houston Astros hurled a no-hitter against the Atlanta Braves in a 6 to 0 win on April 7, 1979. Bob and Ken Forsch were the first brothers to throw no-hitters in the major leagues.

Vernon "Lefty" Gomez of the New York Yankees was the winning pitcher of baseball's first All-Star game. Gomez earned the victory when the American League defeated the National League 4 to 2 in 1933. Lefty Gomez was also the winning pitcher of the 1935 All-Star contest and the 1937 All-Star game.

Pitcher John Nabors of the Philadelphia Athletics lost 19 games in a row. His career record on the mound was 1 win and 24 losses.

Jim Bagby of the Cleveland Indians was the first pitcher to hit a home run in a World Series game. Bagby blasted a round-tripper in Game 5 of the 1920 World Series against the Brooklyn Dodgers. The Indians won the 1920 World Series five games to two.

Early Wynn, who pitched for the Washington Senators, the Cleveland Indians, and the Chicago White Sox, walked 1,775 batters over the course of his 23 year career.

◆

Jim Bunning of the Philadelphia Phillies pitched a perfect game against the New York Mets on June 21, 1964.

◆

Sparky Lyle of the New York Yankees had 35 saves in 1972 to lead the American League.

Special Delivery

Each of the following pitchers was named the Most Valuable Player of the National League. Match each one with the team he pitched for to win the award.

1. Dizzy Dean
(1934 MVP)

A. Brooklyn Dodgers

2. Bucky Walters
(1939 MVP)

B. Philadelphia Phillies

3. Jim Konstanty
(1950 MVP)

C. Cincinnati Reds

4. Don Newcombe
(1956 MVP)

D. St. Louis Cardinals

The correct matches are: 1–D (Dizzy Dean, of the St. Louis Cardinals, was the 1934 MVP); 2–C (Bucky Walters, of the Cincinnati Reds, was the 1939 MVP); 3–B (Jim Konstanty, of the Philadelphia Phillies, was the 1950 MVP); and 4–A (Don Newcombe, of the Brooklyn Dodgers, was the 1956 MVP).

J.R. Richard of the Houston Astros fired six wild pitches in a game on April 10, 1979. Richard also led the National League in strikeouts in 1979 by whiffing 313 batters.

◆

Roscoe Miller of the Detroit Tigers won 20 games as a rookie pitcher in 1901. The very next year, Miller lost 20 games.

◆

Sandy Koufax was a college pitcher at the University of Cincinnati.

◆

Mike Mussina won 17 games and lost 8 while pitching for the New York Yankees in 2003.

◆

Pitcher Dolly Gray of the Washington Senators walked eight batters in one inning on August 28, 1909.

Curt Schilling of the Philadelphia Phillies led the National League in 1997 by striking out 319 batters.

◆

St. Louis Cardinals pitcher Dizzy Dean won 30 games in 1934.

◆

Preacher Roe won 22 games and lost only three while pitching for the Brooklyn Dodgers in 1951.

◆

Pitcher Ralph Terry of the New York Yankees served up 40 home runs to opposing batters in 1962.

◆

Mariano Rivera of the New York Yankees led the American League with 45 saves in 1999.

◆

Mark Langston of the Seattle Mariners led the American League by striking out 262 batters in 1987.

Carl Erskine of the Brooklyn Dodgers struck out 14 New York Yankee batters in a World Series game in 1953. In that contest, Erskine fanned Mickey Mantle four times.

◆

In 1973, pitcher Ken Holtzman of the Chicago Cubs posted a perfect record of 9 wins and 0 losses.

◆

Dan Quisenberry of the Kansas City Royals led the American League in saves five times.

◆

Cy Young won more games than any other pitcher in baseball history with 511. However, Young also lost more games than any other pitcher, 316.

◆

Jim "Catfish" Hunter posted a record of 23 wins and 14 losses while pitching for the New York Yankees in 1975.

Juan Marichal of the San Francisco Giants had 52 shutout wins as a pitcher.

◆

In 1936, pitcher Carl Hubbell of the New York Giants won 16 games in a row.

◆

Jim Palmer of the Baltimore Orioles won the American League's Cy Young Award in 1973, 1975, and 1976.

◆

Hall of Famer Walter Johnson of the Washington Senators was a great pitcher, but he also had control problems. Johnson hit 204 batters over the span of his career.

◆

Harry Gruber of the Cleveland Indians walked 16 batters in a game on April 19, 1890.

On October 8, 1956, Don Larsen of the New York Yankees pitched the first and only (thus far) perfect game in World Series history. Larsen's historic win was over the Brooklyn Dodgers.

◆

Pitcher Pedro Martinez was the Most Valuable Player of the 1999 All-Star game.

◆

While at Washington State University, John Olerud played first base and also pitched. Olerud was named the Baseball America Player of the Year in 1988.

◆

The American League's Cy Young Award winner in 1968 was pitcher Denny McLain of the Detroit Tigers.

◆

In September 1984, New York Mets pitcher Dwight Gooden struck out 32 batters over the course of two consecutive starts. Gooden fanned 16

Pittsburgh Pirates in one start. Five days later, he struck out 16 Philadelphia Phillies in his next start.

◆

While he was at the University of Tennessee, Todd Helton played first base and pitched. He was honored as the Baseball Player of the Year in 1995.

◆

On May 6, 1953, Bobo Holloman of the St. Louis Browns pitched a no-hitter in his very first major league start. Holloman no-hit the Philadelphia Athletics and the Browns won 6 to 0.

◆

San Diego Padres pitcher Chris Young stands six-feet, ten-inches tall and was a standout basketball player at Princeton University.

◆

In his 16 seasons with the New York Giants, pitcher Carl Hubbell averaged less than two walks per nine-inning game.

Tom Seaver won Cy Young Awards in 1969, 1973, and 1975. He struck out 3,640 batters during his 20-year pitching career.

◆

Sandy Koufax of the Los Angeles Dodgers struck out a total of 61 batters in World Series play during his pitching career.

◆

Rookie pitcher Kerry Wood of the Chicago Cubs struck out 20 Houston Astros batters while throwing a one-hitter on May 6, 1998. The Cubs won 2 to 0.

◆

Pitcher Babe Ruth of the Boston Red Sox posted a .087 earned run average in World Series play from 1916 to 1918.

Bob Feller of the Cleveland Indians, who was known as "Rapid Robert" because of the speed of his fastball, pitched three no-hitters and 11 one-hitters during his career.

◆

Whitey Ford of the New York Yankees pitched 146 innings in World Series competition.

◆

Joe "Iron Man" McGinnity of the New York Giants won 31 games on the mound in 1903 and pitched the Giants to 35 wins in 1904. McGinnity won 66 games in just two years.

◆

Dick "The Monster" Radatz of the Red Sox pitched in 79 games for Boston in 1964.

◆

Mark Davis of the San Diego Padres led the National League with 44 saves in 1989.

The Winner's Circle

Lefty Grove won 300 games during his Major League pitching career.

◆

Pitcher Tom Seaver won 311 games during his career.

◆

Don Sutton recorded 324 victories on the mound during his pitching career.

◆

Nolan Ryan won a total of 324 games while pitching in the major leagues.

◆

Grover Cleveland Alexander had 373 career wins as a pitcher in the big leagues.

The New York Yankees' Ron Guidry had a 1.74 ERA in 1978.

◆

John Franco of the New York Mets recorded the 400th save of his career on April 14, 1999 against the Florida Marlins.

◆

Hoyt Wilhelm appeared in 71 games as a rookie pitcher for the New York Giants during the 1952 season.

◆

Johnny VanderMeer of the Cincinnati Reds pitched two consecutive no-hitters. In 1938, VanderMeer no-hit the Boston Braves on June 11, and on June 15 no-hit the Brooklyn Dodgers.

◆

Pitcher Mark Fidrych of the Detroit Tigers was nicknamed "The Bird" because he reminded team-mates of the Big Bird character on *Sesame Street*.

Pitcher Lefty Grove of the Philadelphia Athletics was the Most Valuable Player in the American League in 1931.

◆

Steve Carlton of the Philadelphia Phillies won the Cy Young Award in 1972 with a record of 27 wins and 10 losses.

◆

On October 3, 1968 pitcher Bob Gibson of the St. Louis Cardinals struck out 17 Detroit Tiger batters in game one of the World Series. St. Louis won 4 to 0.

◆

Pitcher Rube Waddel of the Philadelphia Athletics struck out 343 batters during the 1904 season.

◆

In 1916, Grover Cleveland Alexander posted a pitching record of 33 wins and only 12 losses.

Don Drysdale of the Los Angeles Dodgers pitched 58 consecutive scoreless innings in 1968.

◆

Sandy Koufax of the Los Angeles Dodgers struck out 382 batters in 1965.

◆

Bob Feller of the Cleveland Indians struck out 348 batters in 1946.

◆

Dean Chance was the first pitcher from the Anaheim Angels to win a Cy Young Award. Chance was named the top pitcher in the American League in 1964.

◆

Walter Johnson had a total of 417 wins as a big league pitcher. Johnson was nicknamed "The Big Train."

Pitcher Al Benton is the only hurler to face both Babe Ruth and Mickey Mantle. As a member of the Philadelphia Athletics, Benton pitched to Ruth in 1934. Later while playing for the Boston Red Sox, Al Benton pitched to Mickey Mantle in 1952.

◆

John Smoltz of the Atlanta Braves led the National League with 55 saves in 2002.

Throwing the Bull

In June 2006, Cincinnati Reds relief pitcher David Weathers gave up a home run to outfielder Xavier Nady of the New York Mets. The runs ended up costing the Reds a victory. Said Weathers of the pitch Nady hit: "I tried to throw a sinker, and it was as straight as uncooked pasta."

Gaylord Perry had 314 victories on the pitching mound.

◆

Sam McDowell of the Cleveland Indians led the American League by striking out 325 batters in 1965.

◆

Boston Red Sox manager Billy Herman was asked to name the best brush-back pitcher of all time. "Freddie Fitzsimmons is my man," answered Herman. "He once hit me in the on-deck circle."

◆

Hall of Fame pitcher Lefty Gomez said, "The secret of my success was clean living and a fast moving outfield."

Shane Spencer of the New York Mets wore a microphone for the TV broadcast of an interleague game against the New York Yankees. During the contest, Spencer kept muttering about pitches the Yankee hurlers were throwing. "Cutter! Cutter! Fork! Fork!" muttered Spencer for all to hear. Up in the broadcast booth, TV announcer Tim McCarver remarked, "Spencer sounds like a short order cook!"

◆

Hall of Fame pitcher Don Drysdale of the Los Angeles Dodgers was notorious for brushing back batters who crowded the plate. Hall of Fame hitter Ralph Kiner once described the safest way to face the Dodger ace: "The trick in facing Don Drysdale was to hit him before he hit you."

◆

Communist leader Fidel Castro of Cuba aspired to be a big league pitcher, but never made it to the Major Leagues.

CHAPTER 7
Let's Play Catch

asey Stengel, one of baseball's greatest managers and funniest people, said it best when describing the role a catcher has in a game: "A catcher is very important to a team. Without one, you get a lot of passed balls."

The truth is a good catcher is extremely valuable. The catcher is in charge of the infield. The catcher usually calls what type of pitches his batterymate will throw. A catcher has to be tough and durable. Many are also wacky, witty, and more than a little zany. To find out just what we mean, catch up on your reading and move on to this chapter about some of baseball's best backstops.

Backstop Banter:
Roy Campanella

Hall of Fame backstop Roy Campanella of the Brooklyn Dodgers threw out 150 of 200 runners attempting to steal in his first 600 big league games from 1948 to 1952.

Campanella was voted the Most Valuable Player of the National League in 1951, 1953, and 1955.

Campanella's baseball career was cut short by an automobile accident in 1958 which left him paralyzed.

Atlanta Braves catcher Javy Lopez blasted 43 home runs during the 2003 season, good for fourth in the National League.

Carlton Fisk of the Boston Red Sox won AL Rookie of the Year honors in 1972 as a catcher, posting a .293 batting average.

◆

Cleveland Indians catcher Sandy Alomar, Jr. was named the MVP of the 1997 All-Star game.

◆

Ivan "Pudge" Rodriguez was named the Most Valuable Player in the 2003 National League Championship Series while playing catcher for the Florida Marlins.

◆

Catcher Darrell Porter of the St. Louis Cardinals was the Most Valuable Player of the 1982 National League Championship Series.

◆

New York Yankees catcher Bill Dickey played 1,708 games behind the plate.

Backstop Banter: Mike Piazza

Mike Piazza of the San Diego Padres (and other teams) has hit more home runs as a major league catcher than any other player in history. Piazza has clubbed more than 400 homers while playing behind the plate.

Mike Piazza once worked as a batboy for the Los Angeles Dodgers. Tommy Lasorda, the former manager of the Dodgers, was a childhood friend of Mike Piazza's father, Vince Piazza.

In 1988, Major League Baseball teams selected 1,433 players in their annual draft. Mike Piazza was the 1,389th player taken. He was picked by the Los Angeles Dodgers.

Mike Piazza was the 1993 National League Rookie of the Year. That season Piazza batted .318 and smashed 35 home runs. He also drove in 112 runs and was the first NL Rookie of the Year to collect over 100 RBIs in a season.

In 1996, Piazza was named the Most Valuable Player of the All-Star game.

Mike Piazza's first home run as a member of the San Diego Padres came on April 3, 2006, in a 6 to 1 win against the San Francisco Giants.

In 2005, catcher Bengie Molina hit .295 with 15 homers and 69 RBI's for the Anaheim Angels.

◆

Carlton Fisk played 2,499 games and blasted 376 home runs, including 350 homers as a catcher.

◆

Catcher Josh Gibson played for the Pittsburgh Crawfords of the Negro League in 1936, when he clouted 84 home runs.

◆

Catcher Javier Valentin of the Cincinnati Reds had a family reunion at the plate on June 20, 2006, in New York with his older brother, Jose Valentin, the Mets' starting second baseman. In the eighth inning, Jose smashed a ball deep into the outfield and tried to turn it into an inside-the-park home run, but he was tagged out on a close play at home by Javier.

New York Yankees catcher Elston Howard played in 54 World Series games from 1955 to 1967.

◆

In 2002, Benito Santiago was voted the Most Valuable Player of the National League Championship Series while playing catcher for the San Francisco Giants.

◆

Catchers Yogi Berra and Gary Carter both wore No. 8.

◆

In 1942, catcher Mickey Gwen became the first player to hit a pinch-hit homer in an All-Star game.

Backstop Blockade:
It's Your Call

The Atlanta Braves are playing the New York Mets. The game is tied 1 to 1 in the bottom of the 9th inning. The Braves are batting and there is one out with a runner on third base. At the plate is the Atlanta pitcher, who is one of the best bunters in the league. The Braves plan to execute a suicide squeeze play to win the game. Just as the pitcher starts to throw, the Mets' catcher realizes what the Braves are up to. Before the pitcher releases the ball, he steps forward on the plate blocking the batter and preventing him from squaring around. The runner is now headed for home, but the Braves' batter cannot bunt because the Mets' catcher is in his way. The catcher receives the ball and easily tags out the Atlanta runner before he reaches the plate. What is your call?

Answer: The correct call is that the Atlanta Braves runner is safe at home. The run counts and the game is over. The Braves win. The Mets' pitcher is charged with a balk because of what the catcher did. If the game was not over, the run would score and the batter would be awarded first because of interference. The rules of baseball state: If with a runner on third base and trying to score by means of a squeeze play or steal, if the catcher or any other fielder steps on or in front of home base without possession of the ball, or touches the batter or his bat, the pitcher shall be charged with a balk, the batter shall be awarded first base on the interference, and the ball is dead.

On October 3, 2004, Todd Zeile played his last major league game at his original position, catcher. Over the span of his 15-year career, Zeile moved from behind the plate to third and first base. Zeile finished his major league career as a New York Met and homered in his very last at-bat in a contest against the Montreal Expos.

◆

In 1971, catcher Joe Torre of the St. Louis Cardinals led the National League in RBIs, with 137.

◆

Ernie Lombardi of the Cincinnati Reds was the Most Valuable Player of the National League in 1938. The catcher hit .342 with 95 RBIs to win the award.

◆

Catcher Jorge Posada of the New York Yankees does not wear batting gloves.

On July 4, 1976, catcher Tim McCarver of the Philadelphia Phillies lost credit for a grand slam when he passed teammate Garry Maddox on the base path. Despite the base path blunder by the Phillies' backstop, Philadelphia went on to defeat the Pittsburgh Pirates 10 to 5.

◆

Todd Hundley hit a career-high 41 home runs while playing catcher for the New York Mets in 1996.

◆

Paul Lo Duca was the starting catcher for the Los Angeles Dodgers in 2003. That season Lo Duca collected 155 hits in 568 at bats for a .273 batting average.

◆

Mickey Owen had 476 consecutive chances behind the plate without committing an error in 1941, a National League record.

Talk It Up

Casey Stengel, the original manager of the New York Mets, was asked how good his catcher, Choo Choo Coleman, was. Stengel paused for a second and then replied: "Choo Choo is the fastest catcher in the league at running after passed balls."

◆

Early Mets catcher Clarence "Choo Choo" Coleman wasn't a great TV interview. Once, a broadcaster asked him how he got his name. After a long pause, Choo Choo answered, "I don't know."

◆

Catcher-turned-baseball announcer Joe Garagiola received an early scouting report on his speed, which read, "He's a deceiving runner. He's slower than he looks." He stole five bases in his nine-year major league career.

Said Yogi Berra in a tribute to his predecessor Bill Dickey: "Catcher Dickey learned me all of his experience."

Catcher Gene Tenace of the Oakland Athletics was the Most Valuable Player of the 1972 World Series. In that series, Oakland beat the Cincinnati Reds four games to three.

Gabby Hartnett, a catcher for the Chicago Cubs, was named the National League's Most Valuable Player in 1935, when he batted .344 and drove in 91 runs.

Catcher Mickey Cochrane of the Detroit Tigers was the Most Valuable Player of the American League for a second time in 1934. Cochrane batted .320 and had 76 RBI's for Detroit that year.

Catcher Eliezer Alfonzo of the San Francisco Giants homered for his first major league hit on June 3, 2006, in a game against the New York Mets.

◆

Oakland catcher Terry Steinbach was named the Most Valuable Player of the 1988 All-Star game.

◆

In 1970, catcher Johnny Bench of the Cincinnati Reds won the National League home run crown by blasting 45 round-trippers. He also won 10 consecutive Gold Gloves as a catcher from 1968 to 1977.

◆

San Diego Padres catcher Ramon Hernandez hit .290 with 12 home runs and 58 RBIs in 99 games during 2005.

◆

Thurman Munson hit .302 and drove in 105 runs playing catcher for the New York Yankees in 1976, earning MVP honors in the American League.

Backstop Banter: Yogi Berra

As a teenager, Lawrence Peter Berra was signed by the New York Yankees in 1943 to play pro baseball for the sum of 90 dollars a month.

Yogi Berra once played 148 consecutive games behind the plate without committing an error.

Berra collected 71 hits in World Series play, including 17 home runs.

Berra collected 2,150 hits and played in over 2,000 games during his career.

Berra was voted the Most Valuable Player of the American League in 1951, 1954, and 1955.

◆

The wit and wisdom of Hall of Fame catcher Yogi Berra:

"The future ain't what it used to be."

"We made too many wrong mistakes."

"Thank you for making his day necessary."

"He can run anytime he wants to. I'm giving him the red light."

"It gets late early out there."

"I really didn't say everything I said."

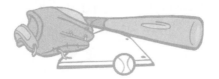

CHAPTER 8
Aye, Aye Skipper

They are the field generals. They make all of the key, on-field decisions. They are big league sports sages who make lineups and decide when to hit and run and when to yank a faltering pitcher. They are all baseball managers, called "skippers" by their players. The skipper guides the team ship in the often turbulent waters of a professional baseball season. It is their task to keep the team ship afloat in the standings. If the team starts to sink, it is almost always the skipper who goes down with his ship.

Big league managers are often wild and wacky. They are cunning and crafty. Most important of all, their job security hinges on one thing . . . winning baseball games!

Joe Torre managed the New York Yankees in 2006. It was Torre's 11th season as New York's manager. Joe Torre has won over 1,000 games as a Yankee skipper.

◆

Manager Connie Mack won 3,731 games and lost 3,948 games during his 53 years as a big league skipper. Mack was born Cornelius McGillicuddy.

◆

Sparky Anderson managed the Cincinnati Reds and the Detroit Tigers. Anderson won 2,194 games during his 26-year career.

Mike Scioscia of the Anaheim Angels was the American League Manager of the Year in 2002.

Tony LaRussa of the St. Louis Cardinals was the National League Manager of the Year in 2002.

Bill McKechnie guided the Pittsburgh Pirates to the World Series crown in 1925. He guided the St. Louis Cardinals to the National League pennant in 1928, and the Cincinnati Reds to National League pennants in 1939 and 1940.

Sparky Anderson's 2,000th win as a manager was a 3 to 2 victory for the Detroit Tigers over the Oakland Athletics on April 15, 1993.

Dusty Baker of the Chicago Cubs was the National League manager of the 2003 All Star game.

Casey at Banter

Casey Stengel managed the Brooklyn Dodgers, the Boston Braves, the New York Yankees and the New York Mets. Casey's career record as a manager was 1,905 wins and 1,842 losses.

Stengel had more World Series wins then any other big league manager. He won 37 World Series games and lost 26.

Hall of Fame pitcher Sandy Koufax said of Casey Stengel: "When I was young and smart, I couldn't understand him. Now that I'm older and dumber, he makes sense to me."

Stengel once told his players to line up alphabetically by height.

When Stengel retired from professional baseball in 1965 he said, "I want to thank all of my players for giving me the honor of being what I was."

Baltimore manager Earl Weaver got his 1,000th career victory on April 5, 1979, when the Orioles beat the Chicago White Sox.

◆

Ralph Houk as a rookie manager with the New York Yankees in 1961 guided them to 109 wins and the World Series title. He finished his managing career with the Boston Red Sox in 1984.

◆

Tony LaRussa was the American League Manager of the Year in 1983 with the Chicago White Sox. In 1988 and 1992, LaRussa was honored as the AL Manager of the Year while he was the skipper of the Oakland A's. LaRussa was the second big league skipper to win manager of the year awards in both the American and National Leagues.

◆

Bucky Harris recorded 2,157 wins as a big league manager from 1924 to 1956.

Dick Williams won 1,571 games and lost 1,451 games as a big league manager from 1967 to 1988.

◆

Bobby Cox was the first big league skipper to be honored with manager of the year awards in both the American and the National Leagues.

◆

Skipper Frank Chance of the Chicago Cubs was the first manager to be ejected from a World Series game. Chance was thrown out by umpire Tom Connolly in the 1910 World Series, which the Philadelphia Athletics won 4 to 1.

◆

Leo "The Lip" Durocher led the New York Giants to a world championship sweep of the Cleveland Indians in 1954.

True or False?

True or false? Tommy Lasorda won more games as a big league manager than Walter Alston.

Answer: False. Walter Alston, who managed the Brooklyn Dodgers and the Los Angeles Dodgers, won 2,040 games as a big league skipper. Tommy LaSorda, who managed the Los Angeles Dodgers, won 1,599 games.

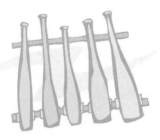

True or false? Joe Torre once managed the Atlanta Braves.

Answer: True. Torre managed the Atlanta Braves from 1982 to 1984. He also managed the New York Mets (1977 to 1981) and the St. Louis Cardinals (1990 to 1995) before taking charge of the New York Yankees in 1996.

◆

True or false? Billy Martin was the manager of the New York Yankees in 1974.

Answer: False. Bill Virdon was the manager of the New York Yankees in 1974. Martin was hired as the Yankees' skipper in 1975.

Manager Jack McKeon of the Florida Marlins won his 1,000th game as a big league skipper on September 3, 2005 when the Marlins beat the New York Mets 5 to 4.

◆

Tony Pena was voted the American League Manager of the Year in 2003 after leading the Kansas City Royals to a record of 83 wins and 79 losses, a year after going 49 and 77. In 2006, Pena worked as a base coach for the New York Yankees.

◆

Former Philadelphia Phillies manager Larry Bowa worked as the third base coach for the New York Yankees in 2006.

◆

Manager Al Lopez guided the Cleveland Indians to 111 wins in 1954. In 1959, Lopez guided the Chicago White Sox to the American League pennant. Lopez, who caught 1,918 games as a major league catcher, was elected to the Hall of Fame as a manager in 1977.

◆

Joe Girardi was the manager of the Florida Marlins during the 2006 baseball season.

◆

Ozzie Guillen of the Chicago White Sox was voted the American League Manager of the Year in 2005. Guillen guided the White Sox to the AL pennant and a World Series championship in 2005.

◆

Boston Red Sox manager Terry Francona was an All American outfielder at the University of Arizona and MVP of the College World Series in 1980.

◆

New York Yankees manager Joe Torre was the National League's batting champion in 1971 when he hit .363 for the St. Louis Cardinals.

Listen to the Manager

Tommy Lasorda, who spent many years as the manager of the Los Angeles Dodgers, said, "The difference between the impossible and the possible lies in a man's determination."

◆

Skipper Leo Durocher of the New York Giants had some interesting insights on how to manage a pitching staff: "You don't save a pitcher for tomorrow. Tomorrow it may rain."

◆

Durocher believed in no-holds-barred baseball. It was Durocher who said, "Nice guys finish last."

◆

Bob Lemon, who managed the Chicago White Sox and the New York Yankees, once said, "Baseball was made for kids, and grownups only screw it up."

Manager Gene Mauch once said: "I'm not the manager because I'm always right, but I'm always right because I'm the manager."

◆

When Yogi Berra was the manager of the New York Yankees he said: "The other teams could make trouble for us if they win."

◆

San Francisco Giants manager Dave Bristol told this to his team after a tough loss. "There'll be two buses leaving the hotel for the park tomorrow. The two o'clock bus will be for those of you who need some extra work. The empty bus will leave at five o'clock."

In 2005, Bobby Bragan of the minor league Fort Worth (Texas) Cats set a record for being the oldest manager of a pro baseball team. Bragan, a former big league skipper, managed the Cats for three innings in a Central League game against Coast Bend before he was ejected for arguing. Bragan was 87 years old when he was tossed from the game. He eclipsed the record formerly held by Connie Mack of the Philadelphia Athletics by eight days.

◆

Gene Mauch managed the California Angels, the Philadelphia Phillies, and the Montreal Expos during his 26 years as a big league skipper. Mauch managed a total of 3,942 games and posted 1,902 victories. He was the National League's Manager of the Year three times.

◆

Gil Hodges was the manager of the 1969 world champion New York Mets.

Winning Numbers

Match the following famous managers with the correct number of games each one won as the skipper of the New York Yankees club:

1. Joe McCarthy
2. Casey Stengel
3. Miller Huggins

A. 1,460 Yankees wins.
B. 1,149 Yankee wins.
C. 1,067 Yankee wins.

The correct matches are: 1–A (Joe McCarthy had 1,460 Yankee wins); 2–B (Casey Stengel had 1,149 Yankee wins); and 3–C (Miller Huggins had 1,067 Yankee wins).

Billy Martin of the Oakland Athletics was the American League Manager of the Year in 1980. Martin guided Oakland to a record of 83 wins and 79 losses in 1980. Martin won his only world championship as the skipper of the 1977 New York Yankees.

◆

On June 6, 1986 manager Steve Boros of the San Diego Padres got tossed out of a game with the Atlanta Braves before the contest even started. The Padres had lost a close game to the Braves the night before because of a disputed call. Boros handed umpire Charlie Williams a videotape of the disputed call to prove his point. Umpire Williams got the point. And manager Boros was ejected before the first pitch was thrown!

◆

Bobby Cox of the Atlanta Braves was voted the National League Manager of the Year in 2005.

Former Brooklyn Dodgers star Cookie Lavagetto managed the Washington Senators.

◆

Jeff Torborg, who managed the Cleveland Indians and other teams, was once the baseball coach at Princeton University.

CHAPTER 9
Batter Up!

Now batting for the Boston Red Sox, Ted Williams.
Now batting for the New York Yankees, Mickey
Mantle. Now batting for the Chicago Cubs, Ernie
Banks. Now batting for the Pittsburgh Pirates,
Roberto Clemente. Aaron! Gwynn! Pujols!
DiMaggio! Yastrzemski! Musial! Garciaparra!
Bonds!

These are the batters who lug the big lumber
up to the plate. They launch rockets that blast out
of the ballpark. These hitters post hefty batting
averages and rack up lots of RBIs. If you're the type
of baseball fan who loves swing music, read on
because we're playing your song!

Official major league batting averages were compiled for the first time in 1865.

◆

Tony Gwynn of the San Diego Padres had 3,141 career hits. Numbered among those hits were 2,378 singles and 543 doubles.

◆

The player who won the National League batting title in 1926 was Bubbles Hargrave of the Cincinnati Reds. Hargrave hit .353.

◆

Dottie Kamenshek was a seven-time All-Star in the All-American Girls Professional Baseball League and collected 1,090 hits during her career.

◆

Mickey Mantle of the New York Yankees is the first player to win baseball's Triple Crown while hitting more than fifty home runs in a season. In 1956, Mantle led the American League with 52 home runs, 130 RBIs, and a .353 batting average.

Honus Wagner of the Pittsburgh Pirates had 252 triples during his 21-year major league career.

◆

Ron Santo hit safely in 28 consecutive games as a member of the Chicago Cubs in 1966.

◆

In 2002, Barry Bonds of the San Francisco Giants won the NL batting title with a .370 average.

◆

Joe "Ducky" Medwick of the St. Louis Cardinals had a National-League best 237 hits in 1937.

◆

Jack Tobin of the St. Louis Browns pounded out 236 hits in the American League in 1921, second by one hit to Harry Heilmann of the Detroit Tigers.

◆

Dom DiMaggio of the Boston Red Sox hit safely in 34 games in a row in 1949.

Nap Lajoie of the Philadelphia Athletics won the Triple Crown in 1901 with 14 home runs, 125 RBIs, and a .426 batting average.

◆

In 1990, Barry Bonds of the Pittsburgh Pirates became the first major leaguer in history to finish a season with at least 30 home runs, 30 stolen bases, 100 RBIs, and a .300 or better batting average.

◆

Paul O'Neill of the New York Yankees hit .359 in 1994 to win the AL batting title.

◆

Frank "Lefty" O'Doul of the Philadelphia Phillies collected 254 hits and had a .398 batting average to top the 1929 National League leaders.

◆

Todd Helton of the Colorado Rockies had 216 hits in 580 at-bats for a healthy .372 batting average, both the best during the 2000 NL season.

Hank Greenberg of the Detroit Tigers had 170 RBIs in 1935, and 183 in 1937, which both topped the American League.

◆

Terry Pendleton of the Atlanta Braves won the NL batting title in 1991 with a .319 average.

◆

In 1989, Ruben Sierra of the Texas Rangers led the American League with 119 RBIs.

◆

Tony Gwynn of the San Diego Padres had a .338 career batting average.

◆

Lastings Milledge of the New York Mets got his first major league hit on May 30, 2006, a double off pitcher Miguel Batista of the Arizona Diamondbacks.

Rico Carty of the Atlanta Braves hit safely in 31 straight games in 1970.

◆

In 1930, New York Yankees star first baseman Lou Gehrig had 171 RBIs, and then 184 the next year. Both times he led the American League.

◆

Johnny Frederick of the Brooklyn Dodgers had nine pinch hits in 1932, and six of them were home runs!

The first New York Yankees player to win the Triple Crown was Lou Gehrig. In 1934, Gehrig led all American League hitters with a .363 batting average, 49 home runs, and 165 RBIs.

◆

In 1965, the Los Angeles Dodgers had an infield made up of all switch hitters. The switch hitters included first baseman Wes Parker, second baseman Jim "Junior" Gilliam, shortstop Maury Wills, and third baseman Jim LeFebvre.

◆

Luke Appling of the Chicago White Sox batted .388 in 1936, best in the American League.

◆

Roberto Clemente won four National League batting titles. Clemente led the NL in 1961 with a .351 average, in 1964 with .339, in 1965 with .329, and in 1967 with .357.

The 400 Club

Bill Terry of the New York Giants won the National League batting title in 1930 by posting a .401 batting average.

◆

In 1941, Ted Williams of the Boston Red Sox batted .406 to win the American League batting title. That same season, Williams clouted 37 homes runs and drove in 120 runs. Amazingly, he struck out only 27 times the entire season.

◆

Harry Heilmann of the Detroit Tigers hit .403 in 1923 to win the batting title of the American League. Heilman had 211 hits in 524 at-bats, including 44 doubles, 11 triples, and 18 home runs. He also had 115 RBIs.

Nap Lajoie of the Philadelphia Athletics posted the highest batting average in the history of the American League. In 1901, Lajoie hit .426 by banging out 232 hits in 544 at-bats, including 48 doubles, 14 triples and 14 home runs.

◆

Ty Cobb of the Detroit Tigers hit over .400 for two consecutive seasons. In 1911, Cobb had 248 hits in 591 at-bats for a .420 batting average. In 1912, Cobb smashed 226 hits in 553 at-bats for a .409 batting average.

◆

Rogers Hornsby of the St. Louis Cardinals was the first National Leaguer to record a batting average of .400 or better. In 1922, Hornsby collected 250 hits in 623 at-bats for a .401 batting average.

Hornsby had 227 hits in 536 at-bats in 1924 for a .424 batting average. Hornsby's hits included 43 doubles, 14 triples and 25 home runs.

In 1925, Rogers Hornsby had a .403 batting average, which was tops in the National League. Hornsby had 203 hits in 504 at-bats, including 41 doubles, 10 triples, and 39 home runs.

Shoeless Joe Jackson hit .408 in 1911. Jackson smacked 233 hits in 571 at-bats that season including 45 doubles, 19 triples, and 7 home runs.

Myril Hoag of the New York Yankees had six singles in a game against the Boston Red Sox on June 6, 1934.

◆

Sammy Sosa of the Chicago Cubs had a National-League best 160 RBIs during the 2001 season.

◆

In 1954, Ted Kluszewski of the Cincinnati Reds led the National League with 141 RBIs.

◆

In 2000, Nomar Garciaparra of the Boston Red Sox won the AL batting crown with a .372 average.

◆

Jose Valentin got his first hit as a member of the New York Mets on April 20, 2006, in a game against the San Diego Padres.

Fernando Tatis of the St. Louis Cardinals had 8 RBIs in one inning of a game played on April 23, 1999, courtesy of two grand slams.

◆

The Philadelphia Phillies' Chuck Klein touched opposing pitchers for 250 hits during the 1930 National League season.

◆

Hugh Duffy of the Boston Beaneaters won the Triple Crown in 1894 with a .440 batting average, 18 home runs, and 145 RBIs.

◆

In 1962, Tommy Davis of the Los Angeles Dodgers had 153 RBIs, tops in the National League.

◆

Andre Dawson of the Chicago Cubs drove in 137 runs in 1987 to lead the National League.

Hall of Famer Jimmie Foxx drove in 1,922 runs during his 20-year big league career.

◆

Mickey Vernon of the Washington Senators won American League batting crowns in 1946 with a .353 average, and in 1953 with .337.

◆

Carl Yastrzemski of the Boston Red Sox won the Triple Crown in 1967 thanks to a .326 batting average, 121 RBIs, and 44 home runs.

◆

Tony Oliva of the Minnesota Twins collected an American-League best 217 hits in 161 games as a rookie batter in 1964.

◆

Ron Northey of the Chicago White Sox was 15 for 39 as a pinch hitter in 1956.

In 1969, Cleon Jones of the New York Mets posted a .340 batting average. In 1970, Jones hit safely in 23 straight games.

◆

Ichiro Suzuki of the Seattle Mariners won the American League's batting title in 2001 with a .350 average.

◆

Joe DiMaggio of the New York Yankees won back to back American League batting titles hitting .381 in 1939 and .352 in 1940.

◆

George Sisler of the St. Louis Browns smacked a MLB-record 257 hits in a 154-game season in 1920.

◆

Gus Bell collected the first hit in the history of the New York Mets franchise, on April 11, 1962.

Jimmie Foxx of the Philadelphia Athletics had an American-League-best 169 RBIs during the 1932 season. In 1938, while playing for the Boston Red Sox, Foxx drove in 175 runs, again best in the American League.

◆

Bob Meusel of the New York Yankees hit for the cycle (single, double, triple, and home run) in a game three times, in 1921, 1922, and 1928.

◆

Willie Wilson of the Kansas City Royals led the American League with a .332 batting average in 1982.

◆

Alex Johnson of the California Angels had 202 hits in 1970.

◆

Earle Combs of the New York Yankees had 231 hits during the 1927 season, tops in the American League.

3,000 Hit Clubbers

Paul Molitor was the first major leaguer to smash a triple for his 3,000th career hit. Molitor's milestone hit came on September 16, 1996.

Carl Yastrzemski's 3,000th hit was a single off New York Yankees pitcher Jim Beattie on September 12, 1979.

Pete Rose's 3,000th career hit was a single off Montreal Expos' pitcher Steve Rogers on May 5, 1978. On April 13, 1984, Rose smacked the 4,000th hit of his career. It was a double off Philadelphia Phillies pitcher Jerry Koosman. Rose had an astounding total of 4,256 hits during his 24-year career.

Stan Musial's 3,000th hit was a pinch-hit double off pitcher Moe Drabowsky of the Chicago Cubs on May 13, 1958.

◆

Al Kaline of the Detroit Tigers had 3,007 hits in a major league career from 1953 to 1974.

◆

Rod Carew of the Minnesota Twins had 3,053 hits in his big league career from 1967 to 1985.

◆

Tony Gwynn of the San Diego Padres collected his 3,000th career hit on August 6, 1999, a single off pitcher Dan Smith of the Montreal Expos.

Dave Winfield got his 3,000th career hit on September 16, 1993, a single off pitcher Dennis Eckersley. Winfield played for the San Diego Padres, New York Yankees, California Angels, and other teams, and had 3,110 hits before retiring in 1995.

On May 17, 1925, Tris Speaker of the Cleveland Indians collected his 3,000th career hit off hurler Tom Zachary of the Washington Senators.

George Brett played major league baseball for 21 years and achieved 3,154 hits.

Carl Yastrzemski amassed a total of 3,419 hits during his big league career from 1961 to 1983.

Lou Brock pounded out 3,023 hits during his 19-year baseball career.

Rafael Palmeiro of the Baltimore Orioles collected his 3,000th hit of his career, a double off pitcher Joel Pineiro of the Seattle Mariners on July 15, 2005. Palmeiro became the fourth player to have 3,000 or more hits and 500 or more home runs.

Hank Aaron's 3,000th hit was an infield single off pitcher Wayne Simpson of the Cincinnati Reds on May 17, 1970. Aaron had 3,771 hits and 755 home runs during his 23-year major league career to 1976.

Willie Mays had 3, 283 hits and 660 home runs during his 23-year big league baseball career.

◆

Eddie Murray amassed 3,255 hits and 504 home runs during his 21-year career.

◆

Cal Ripken, Jr. of the Baltimore Orioles singled off Minnesota Twins pitcher Hector Carrasco on April 15, 2000 for the 3,000th hit of his career. Ripken played 21 years of major league baseball and stroked 3,184 hits.

◆

Stan Musial of the St. Louis Cardinals collected 3,630 hits during his 22-year career.

◆

Ty Cobb had 4,189 hits in his 24-year career.

3,000 Hit Club Quiz

Which of the following players, all of whom blasted 3,000 or more hits during their careers, was not a left-handed batter? Is it: (A) Eddie Collins, (B) Paul Waner, (C) Tris Speaker, or (D) Paul Molitor?

Answer: (D) Molitor, who had 3,319 career hits. Molitor was a right-handed batter. Collins (3,315 hits), Waner (3,152 hits), and Speaker (3,514 hits) were all left-handed batters.

True or false? Eddie Murray (3,255 hits), Pete Rose (4,256 hits) and Honus Wagner (3,415 hits) were all switch hitters.

Answer: False. Murray and Rose were switch hitters, but Wagner was strictly a right-handed batter.

Not Bogged Down

Wade Boggs finished his major league baseball career with a total of 3,010 hits.

◆

Wade Boggs' 3,000th career hit was a home run off pitcher Chris Haney of the Cleveland Indians on August 6, 1999. Boggs was the first major league player in history to smash a home run for his 3,000th hit. He kissed home plate.

◆

Boggs posted a .328 career batting average. He played in 2,439 big league games during his 18-year career.

Rusty Staub hit .333 for the Houston Astros in 1967.

◆

John Paciorek batted .1000 for his major league career. In 1963, Paciorek went 3 for 3 as a batter in one game for the Houston Astros. Paciorek never batted again in the major leagues and thus finished his career with a .1000 batting average.

◆

In 2001, Bret Boone of the Seattle Mariners led the American League with 141 RBIs.

Yankee Hit Men

Babe Ruth had 2,873 career hits.

Derek Jeter collected his 2,000th hit against the Kansas City Royals on May 26, 2006.

Lou Gehrig had 2,721 career hits.

Yogi Berra had 2,150 hits in his career.

Bernie Williams hammered out his 2,000th career hit on June 10, 2004 against the Colorado Rockies.

Don Mattingly collected 2,153 hits playing for the New York Yankees.

Mickey Mantle had 2,415 hits.

Todd Zeile of the New York Mets collected the 2,000th hit of his career on September 19, 2004 in a game against the Pittsburgh Pirates. Zeile's hit was a single off pitcher Jose Mesa.

◆

Albert Belle of the Chicago White Sox had 152 RBIs in 1998.

◆

"Wee" Willie Keeler played 19 years in the major leagues and had a .341 career batting average. In 1897, Keeler hit safely in 44 straight games.

◆

Bill Mueller of the Boston Red Sox was the American League's batting champion in 2003, posting a .326 average.

◆

Manny Mota had 150 pinch hits during his 20-year baseball career.

Felix Millan hit 37 doubles as a New York Met in 1975.

◆

Alex Rodriguez collected 201 hits in 632 at-bats to hit .318 as a shortstop for the Texas Rangers in 2001.

◆

On August 4, 1982 Joel Youngblood played for two different major league teams in two different cities and got hits for both teams. In the afternoon, Youngblood got a double for the New York Mets in a game against the Chicago Cubs. After the game, Youngblood was traded to the Montreal Expos. In the evening, he got a single against the Philadelphia Phillies.

◆

George Foster of the Cincinnati Reds had 149 RBIs during the 1977 season. He led the National League in RBIs in 1976, 1977, and 1978.

Al Simmons of the Philadelphia Athletics hammered out 253 hits in 1925, topping the American League.

◆

Boston Red Sox star outfielder Ted Williams had 163 hits in 420 at-bats for a .388 batting average in 1957.

◆

In 1930, Hack Wilson of the Chicago Cubs drove in 191 runs, best in the National League.

◆

Dave Parker of the Pittsburgh Pirates won back-to-back National League batting titles in 1977 with a .338 average, and in 1978 with a .334 average.

◆

Smoky Burgess had a career total of 145 pinch hits.

The Georgia Peach: A Sweet Hitter

Ty Cobb of the Detroit Tigers put together many great consecutive game hitting streaks. In 1911, Ty Cobb hit safely in 40 consecutive games, a Detroit record. He had a 35-game hitting streak in 1917.

◆

In 1909, Ty Cobb won the Triple Crown. Cobb led all American League hitters with a .377 batting average, 107 RBIs, and 9 home runs.

◆

Ty Cobb got five or more hits in a game 14 times during his major league career. In 1922, Cobb got five or more hits in one game four times.

◆

Ty Cobb hit 295 triples, achieving a season best of 24 twice in 1911 and 1918.

Sam Crawford of the Detroit Tigers had a total of 309 triples during his 19-year career.

◆

Rogers Hornsby of the St. Louis Cardinals was the first player to win the National League's Triple Crown two times. In 1922, Hornsby batted .401, drove in 152 runs, and hit 42 home runs. In 1925, he had a .403 batting average, 143 RBIs, and 39 home runs.

◆

Carl Yastrzemski went 2 for 3 in the 3,000th game of his major league career. The Boston Red Sox star smacked two singles against the Cleveland Indians in his 3,000th big league contest in May 1981.

◆

Frank Thomas of the Chicago White Sox won the batting title of the American League in 1997 with a .347 average.

Willie Mays of the San Francisco Giants had a career-best 20 triples in 1957.

◆

Ted Williams of the Boston Red Sox was the first player to win the Triple Crown in the American League two times. In 1942, Williams had 36 homers, 137 RBIs, and a .356 batting average. In 1947, he recorded 32 homers, 114 RBIs, and a .343 batting average.

◆

Stan Musial won the National League batting title seven times, in 1943 (.357), 1946 (.365), 1948 (.376), 1950 (.346), 1951 (.355), 1952 (.336), and 1957 (.351).

◆

Joe "Ducky" Medwick of the St. Louis Cardinals captured baseball's elusive Triple Crown in 1937, with a .374 batting average, 154 RBIs, and 31 home runs.

Babe Herman of the Brooklyn Dodgers hit for the cycle (single, double, triple, and home run all in the same game) three times in 1931.

◆

In 1999, Mark McGwire led the National League with 147 RBIs.

◆

Greg Luzinski of the Philadelphia Phillies led the National League in RBIs with 120 in 1975.

◆

In 1955, Duke Snider of the Brooklyn Dodgers had 136 RBIs to lead the National League.

◆

Babe Ruth had a .393 batting average for the New York Yankees in 1923, the year he won his only league MVP award.

◆

Tommie Agee had 61 extra base hits for the New York Mets in 1970.

Stan "The Man" Musial of the St. Louis Cardinals had 725 doubles during his major league career.

◆

Bill Buckner of the Chicago Cubs led the National League in hitting in 1980 with a .324 average.

◆

Cecil Fielder of the Detroit Tigers led the American League in RBIs from 1990 to 1992. Fielder had 132 in 1990, 133 in 1991, and 124 in 1992.

◆

The first time there were Triple Crown winners in the National and American Leagues at the same time was 1933. Chuck Klein of the Philadelphia Phillies won the National League crown with a .368 batting average, 28 home runs, and 120 RBIs. The American League crown winner was also from a Philadelphia area team. Jimmie Foxx of the Philadelphia Athletics had a .356 batting average, 48 home runs, and 163 RBIs.

Johnny Bench of the Cincinnati Reds drove in 1,013 runs from 1970 to 1979.

◆

Willie Stargell of the Pittsburgh Pirates had 119 RBIs during the 1973 season to lead the National League in that category.

◆

Babe Herman of the Brooklyn Dodgers had 241 hits in 614 at bats during the 1930 National League season.

◆

Tony Gwynn of the San Diego Padres hit a National-League-best .394 in 1994.

◆

Frank Robinson of the Baltimore Orioles won the Triple Crown in 1966, leading the American League in batting average (.316), home runs (49), and RBIs (122).

Rod Carew of the Minnesota Twins hit 80 triples from 1970 to 1979.

◆

Dottie Schroeder played 12 seasons in the All-American Girls Professional Baseball League and drove in a league-high 431 runs.

◆

Bob Watson was the first major league player to hit for the cycle in the National and American Leagues, on June 24, 1977, for the National League's Houston Astros, and on September 15, 1979, for the Boston Red Sox.

◆

Hall of Fame catcher Bill Dickey of the New York Yankees had a career-best .362 batting average in 1936.

◆

In 1958, Ernie Banks of the Chicago Cubs led the National League with 129 RBIs. In 1959, Banks again led the NL with 143 RBIs.

Shawn Green of the Toronto Blue Jays hit 35 home runs and stole 35 bases in 1998.

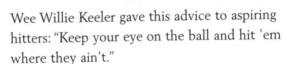
Parting Shots

Wee Willie Keeler gave this advice to aspiring hitters: "Keep your eye on the ball and hit 'em where they ain't."

Ping Brodie of the Chicago White Sox described what it was like to bat against fireballer Walter Johnson of the Washington Senators: "You can't hit what you can't see."

Yogi Berra had this to say about Frank Robinson's hitting style: "If you can't copy him, don't imitate him."

Hank Aaron once made this comparison between two sports: "It took me seventeen years to get 3,000 hits in baseball. I did it in one afternoon at the golf course."

◆

Pitcher Lefty Gomez had this to say about hitter Jimmy Foxx: "Jimmie Foxx is so strong he even has muscles in his hair."

CHAPTER 10
Kings of Clout

Crack! Zoom! See ya! It's outta' here! In baseball, there is nothing like the thrill of watching a big league slugger launch a moon shot into the upper deck of a ballpark. Some fans call it a dinger. To others it's a round-tripper or a four-sacker. Occasionally, it's even dubbed a grand salami if it's hit when the bases are full. No matter how you describe it, a home run in baseball is the icing on the cake. It's the mustard on the hotdog. It adds that unique flavor to the game of baseball.

On the following pages, you can read all about the players who send those sonic blasts into the distant bleachers. These ballplayers are baseball's kings of clout.

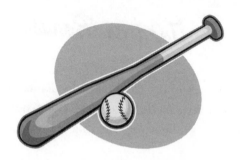

Travis Hafner of the Cleveland Indians was the first player in major league history to smash five grand slams before baseball's All-Star break. Hafner performed his historic home run feat in 2006.

◆

Hank Aaron hit 755 home runs during his major league career.

◆

Babe Ruth hit 714 home runs during his major league career.

Good as Bonds

Barry Bonds of the San Francisco Giants smashed 73 home runs in 2001 to establish a major league record for the most homers in a season.

Bonds hit his 500th home run off Terry Adams of the Los Angeles Dodgers on April 17, 2001.

Bonds hit the 715th home run of his career on May 28, 2006 off pitcher Byung-hyun Kim of the Colorado Rockies.

In 1954, Joanne Weaver hit .429 and blasted 29 home runs while playing in the All-American Girls Professional Baseball League.

♦

Jackie Robinson's only home run in All-Star play came in the first inning of the 1952 game.

♦

Steve Garvey of the Los Angeles Dodgers hit four home runs in the 1978 National League playoffs.

♦

Hall of Fame pitcher Warren Spahn hit 35 home runs before he retired in 1965.

♦

On June 3, 2006, Damion Easley of the Arizona Diamondbacks hit three home runs in a game against the Atlanta Braves.

Alex Rodriguez was the youngest major leaguer to hit 400 home runs. Rodriguez was 29 years old when he blasted his 400th home run playing for the New York Yankees in a game against the Milwaukee Brewers on June 8, 2005.

◆

Ted Williams of the Boston Red Sox hit three home runs in a game against the Cleveland Indians on June 13, 1957. That year, Williams became the first American Leaguer to have two three-home-run games in a season.

◆

Joe Adcock of the Milwaukee Braves hit four home runs and a double with a borrowed bat in a game on July 31, 1954.

Gary Sheffield his 400th home run of his career while playing for the New York Yankees on July 27, 2004. Sheffield's blast came against pitcher Michael Nakamura of the Toronto Blue Jays in a 7 to 4 New York victory.

◆

John "Boog" Powell hit three home runs in one game three times during his career. He did it in 1963, 1964, and 1966. Powell's three round trippers in 1963 were on consecutive at-bats.

The Shot Heard Around the World

In 1951, the Brooklyn Dodgers and the New York Giants finished the regular seasons tied in the standings and were forced to play a three-game playoff to determine the winner of the National League pennant. The Giants won the first game 3 to 1. The Dodgers won the second game 10 to 0.

The third and deciding game of the series was played at New York's Polo Grounds on October 3. The Dodgers took a 4 to 1 lead into the bottom of the ninth inning. Alvin Dark singled for the Giants to lead off. Don Mueller then singled Dark to third. Monte Irvin popped out for out number one. Whitey Lockman then bashed a double, which made the score 4 to 2 in

Brooklyn's favor, but the Giants still had runners on second and third.

Ralph Branca came in to pitch for the Dodgers. Bobby Thompson was the Giants' hitter. Branca's first pitch was a called strike. His second pitch would have been a strike. Thompson swung and launched the baseball into the stands for a 5 to 4 Giants win over the Dodgers and the National League pennant.

"The Giants win the pennant! The Giants win the pennant!" screamed radio broadcaster Russ Hodges over the air waves.

It was one of big league baseball's most memo rable moments. Thompson's hit was one of the game's most amazing home runs. In fact to this day, it was remembered by sports fans as "The shot heard round the world."

Willie Mays of the San Francisco Giants hit 17 home runs in the month of August in 1965, a National League record.

◆

On April 30, 1961, Mays hit four home runs in a game against the Milwaukee Braves.

◆

Mays had 63 games where he hit two or more home runs in a single contest.

◆

On July 13, 1971, Reggie Jackson of the American League hit a home run off pitcher Dock Ellis in the All-Star game estimated to have traveled 650 feet!

◆

When Joe Torre won his 1,000th game as a New York Yankees skipper on May 7, 2006, outfielder Hideki Matsui hit a three-run homer in the 8 to 5 victory over the Texas Rangers.

Al Rosen of the Cleveland Indians hit 37 home runs as a rookie in 1950.

◆

Frank Robinson hit an American-League-leading 49 home runs playing for the Baltimore Orioles in 1966.

◆

Edwin Donald "Duke" Snider of the Brooklyn Dodgers was the first player to hit four home runs in a World Series twice. Snider did it in 1952 and 1955 against the New York Yankees.

◆

Lastings Milledge of the New York Mets hit his first major league home run off Armando Benitez of the San Francisco Giants on June 4, 2006.

◆

Ernie Banks of the Chicago Cubs hit five grand Slams in 1955.

Catcher Roy Campanella of the Brooklyn Dodgers hit 41 home runs in 1953.

◆

In 1936, Tony Lazzeri of the New York Yankees hit six home runs over a span of three consecutive games.

◆

Willie McCovey of the San Francisco Giants hit three consecutive home runs in a game twice. McCovey connected for three homers in a row on September 22, 1963, and again on April 22, 1964.

In 1965, the Los Angeles Dodgers won the National League pennant even though they hit only 78 total home runs.

◆

Tino Martinez of the New York Yankees hit five home runs in five straight games in 2005.

Don Mattingly of the New York Yankees hit home runs in eight straight games in 1987.

◆

In 1999, Edgar Martinez of the Seattle Mariners hit five home runs in two games.

◆

Reggie Jackson hit only one home run as a rookie with the Kansas City Athletics in 1967. Jackson went on to clout 563 homers during his 21-year career.

Crown the NL Home Run Kings

Match each of the following sluggers with the correct year he won a home run crown and the number of homers he clouted that season:

1. Jim Thome
   (Philadelphia Phillies)

   A. 1991 (38 homers)

2. Matt Williams
   (San Francisco Giants)

   B. 1994 (43 homers)

3. Duke Snider
   (Brooklyn Dodgers)

   C. 1951 (42 homers)

4. Dante Bichette
   (Colorado Rockies)

   D. 1956 (43 homers)

5. Ralph Kiner
   (Pittsburgh Pirates)

   E. 1995 (40 homers)

6. Sammy Sosa
   (Chicago Cubs)

   F. 2003 (47 homers)

7. Howard Johnson
   (New York Mets)

   G. 2002 (49 homers)

Bucky Dent of the New York Yankees hit a three-run homer off pitcher Mike Torrez of the Boston Red Sox in a one-game AL East playoff on October 2, 1978, at Boston's Fenway Park. Dent's dinger gave the Yanks a 5 to 4 win and division title.

◆

Chicago Cubs shortstop Ernie Banks hit 500th home run of his career on May 12, 1970 against pitcher Pat Jarvis of the Atlanta Braves.

◆

Scott Seabol of the St. Louis Cardinals hit the first home run of his major league career in a game against the New York Yankees on June 12, 2005.

Gil Hodges of the Brooklyn Dodgers hit four home runs in one game on August 31, 1950.

◆

On August 27, 1974, Benny Ayala of the New York Mets hit a home run in his first major league at-bat in a game against the Houston Astros.

◆

Babe Ruth hit his 120th career home run off of Jim Bagby of the Cleveland Indians on June 10, 1921. At the time, the round-tripper made Ruth baseball's all-time home run leader.

◆

In 1947, Ralph Kiner of the Pittsburgh Pirates hit eight home runs over a span of four consecutive games.

◆

Bobby Bonds of the San Francisco Giants hit a grand slam in his first major league game on June 25, 1968.

Roger Maris hit a total of 275 home runs during his 12-year career.

◆

Joe Morgan of the Cincinnati Reds was the first player in major league history to hit 200 home runs and steal 600 bases.

◆

Rocky Colavito of the Cleveland Indians hit home runs in the 1959, 1961, and 1962 All-Star games.

◆

Ken Griffey, Jr. hit the 550th home run of his baseball career on June 27, 2006 off Kansas City Royals pitcher Mike Ward.

Bobby Bonds of the California Angels smashed 37 homers and swiped 41 bases in 1977.

◆

Hall of Fame catcher Johnny Bench hit 389 home runs as a player for the Cincinnati Reds.

◆

Babe Ruth hit the last home runs of his career while playing for the Boston Braves. He smashed home runs 712, 713, and 714 in a game against the Pittsburgh Pirates played on May 25, 1935.

◆

In 1968, Frank Howard of the Washington Senators hit ten home runs during a span of 20 at-bats.

◆

Shortstop Rico Petrocelli of the Boston Red Sox hit 40 home runs in 1969.

◆

Jeff Bagwell of the Houston Astros hit 43 home runs and stole 31 bases in 1997.

Crown the AL Home Run Kings

Match each of the following sluggers with the correct year he won a home run crown and the number of homers he clouted that season.

1. Mark McGwire
   (Oakland Athletics)

2. Greg Nettles
   (New York Yankees)

3. Larry Doby
   (Cleveland Indians)

4. Fred McGriff
   (Toronto Blue Jays)

5. Ken Griffey, Jr.
   (Seattle Mariners)

6. Roy Sievers
   (Washington Senators)

7. Frank Howard
   (Washington Senators)

A. 1976 (32 homers)

B. 1954 (32 homers)

C. 1957 (42 homers)

D. 1968 (44 homers)

E. 1996 (52 homers)

F. 1989 (36 homers)

G. 1999 (48 homers)

Dale Long of the Pittsburgh Pirates hit home runs in eight consecutive games in 1956.

Mickey Mantle hit the 536th and last home run of his career on September 20, 1968. It was a solo shot off Jim Lonborg of the Boston Red Sox.

Ty Cobb and Rusty Staub were the first two major leaguers to hit home runs as teenagers and players past their 40th birthdays.

Nate Colbert of the San Diego Padres hit five home runs in a doubleheader on August 1, 1972.

Harmon Killebrew of the Minnesota Twins hit home runs in the 1961, 1965, and 1971 All-Star games.

◆

In 1958, pitcher Don Drysdale of the Los Angeles Dodgers smacked seven home runs in 47 games.

◆

On July 5, 1993, Ricky Henderson of the Oakland Athletics led off both games of a doubleheader with a home run.

◆

Ted Williams hit his 521st home run in his last major league at-bat. Williams homered for the Boston Red Sox in a game against the Baltimore Orioles on September 28, 1960.

◆

Jim Wynn hit 37 homer runs for the Houston Astros in 1967.

Rick Wise of the Philadelphia Phillies was the first major league pitcher to hit two home runs in a game while throwing a no-hitter. Wise clouted two dingers in a no-hit performance against the Cincinnati Reds on June 23, 1971.

◆

George Foster of the Cincinnati Reds won NL home run crowns in 1977 and 1978. Foster crashed 52 homers in 1977 and smashed 40 homers in 1978.

◆

In 1974, Dick Allen of the Chicago White Sox won the American League home run title by bashing 32 homers.

◆

Dave Kingman of the Chicago Cubs hit 48 homers in 1979 to win the National League home run crown.

Aaron Boone's 11th inning home run in Game Seven of the 2003 American League Championship Series enabled the New York Yankees to beat the Boston Red Sox and to capture the ALCS crown.

◆

Barry Bonds hit the 700th home run of his career on September 17, 2004 off pitcher Jake Peavy of the San Diego Padres.

◆

Stan Musial of the St. Louis Cardinals hit five home runs in a doubleheader on May 2, 1954.

◆

Slugger Carl Yastrzemski of the Boston Red Sox hit his 400th career home run off Mike Morgan of the Oakland Athletics on July 24, 1979.

◆

Jose Conseco of the Oakland A's hit 42 homers to win the AL home run crown in 1988.

Mickey Mantle hit the 500th home run of his career on May 14, 1967. The blast came off Baltimore Orioles pitcher Stu Miller and gave Mantle's New York Yankees a 6 to 5 victory.

◆

St. Louis Cardinals slugger Mark McGwire hit his 62nd home run of the 1998 baseball season on September 8, surpassing the record of 61 in a season set by New York Yankees star Roger Maris in 1961. McGwire's record-breaking bomb was hit off pitcher Steve Trachsel of the Chicago Cubs. Mark McGwire went on to hit 70 home runs that season.

◆

Jimmy Foxx, who blasted 534 homers during his 20-year career, hit only one home run in All-Star competition, in 1935.

Grand Slam Salute

New York Yankees first baseman Lou Gehrig hit a total of 23 grand slams.

Jimmie Foxx belted 17 grand slams.

Ted Williams blasted 17 grand slams.

Babe Ruth clouted 16 grand slams.

Hank Aaron cracked 16 grand slams.

Gil Hodges stroked 14 grand slams.

Willie McCovey smacked 18 grand slams.

Joe DiMaggio and Ralph Kiner each hit 13 grand slams.

CHAPTER 11
Take One for the Team

Go Mets! Go Yankees! Go Red Sox, White Sox and Dodgers! Part of the fun of being a baseball fan is rooting for your favorite team. It doesn't matter if you're wild about the Reds or the Rangers. It's not important if you think the Tigers are terrific or the Braves are the best ever.

This chapter has fun facts and tantalizing tid bits about every major league club, so there should be something of interest in here for everyone from Philadelphia to San Diego and from Toronto to Tampa Bay. So what are you waiting for? Let's go team!

ANAHEIM ANGELS

◆

The Angels entered the American League in 1961.

◆

Albie Pearson was the first full-time Angels player to bat over .300 when he hit .304 in 1963.

◆

Pitcher Nolan Ryan of the Angels shut out eight different teams during the 1972 season.

◆

In July 1991, pitcher Jim Abbott of the Angels defeated mound rival Scott Kamieniecki of the New York Yankees 8 to 4. Kamieniecki won an earlier matchup the previous month. The pair were roommates at the University of Michigan.

ARIZONA DIAMONDBACKS

The name Diamondbacks was selected in a poll of Arizona baseball fans.

Luis Gonzalez of the Diamondbacks had a .336 batting average in 1999. He also had 206 hits, which was tops in the National League that season.

Tony Womack of the Diamondbacks led the National League in stolen bases in 1999 with 72 steals.

In 2000, pitcher Randy Johnson of the Diamondbacks stuck out a career high 347 batters.

Carlos Baerga led the Diamondbacks with a .343 batting average in 2003.

ATLANTA BRAVES

◆

The Braves played in Boston from 1871 to 1952. They played in Milwaukee from 1953 to 1965 and then moved to Atlanta.

◆

Home run king Hank Aaron of the Braves did not always wear 44. In 1954, when Aaron was a rookie player, he wore 5 for one year.

◆

Pitcher Joey Jay was the first graduate of Little League to make it to the major leagues. Jay became a member of the Milwaukee Braves in 1953 and eventually won 99 games as a major league hurler.

◆

Atlanta's Chipper Jones tied a major league record by getting an extra-base hit in 14 straight games on July 16, 2006. Jones' home run tied the record set in 1927 by Paul Waner of the Pittsburgh Pirates.

BALTIMORE ORIOLES

◆

On June 10, 1892, catcher Wilbert Robinson of the Orioles has 11 RBIs in a single game.

◆

Joe Altobelli managed the Baltimore Orioles to a World Series Championship in 1983. The Orioles beat the Philadelphia Phillies four games to one game in the series.

◆

Skipper Frank Robinson of the Baltimore Orioles was an American League manager of the Year in 1989.

◆

Dave Philley had 24 pinch hits for the Baltimore Orioles in 1961.

◆

Cal Ripkin, Jr. of the Baltimore Orioles played in more consecutive major league games than any other player in history. Ripkin played 2,632 straight games.

BOSTON RED SOX

The Red Sox were original members of the American League. The Red Sox have been in the AL since it was formed in 1901.

The Red Sox played a 24-inning game against the Philadelphia Athletics on September 1, 1906. Philadelphia beat Boston 4 to 1.

Boston's Fenway Park opened in 1912.

In 1916, the Red Sox beat the Brooklyn Dodgers to win their second straight World Series.

The 2004 Red Sox were the first World Series winners to be featured on a Wheaties cereal box since the 1999 New York Yankees.

Jason Varitek caught his 990th game for the Red Sox on July 16, 2006.

CHICAGO CUBS

◆

The Chicago Cubs are the only club to hold a franchise continuously from the beginning of the National League in 1876 up to the present.

◆

Over the years, the Cubs have been known as the White Stockings, the Colts, and the Orphans. In 1900, they became the Cubs.

◆

Bill Dahlen of the old Colts hit safely in 42 straight games in 1894.

◆

Phil Wrigley, the owner of the Cubs, founded the All-American Girls Professional League in 1943.

CHICAGO WHITE SOX

◆

Shoeless Joe Jackson of the White Sox batted .408 in 1911, .395 in 1912, and .373 in 1913. He had a .356 career batting average and 1,772 career hits, but because of his involvement in the 1919 World Series betting scandal, he is not in baseball's Hall of Fame.

◆

In 1943, 30-year-old-rookie Guy Curthright of the White Sox got a hit in his first major league game. Curthright went on to hit safely in his first 26 big league contests.

◆

The White Sox play their home games at Comiskey Park.

CINCINNATI REDS

◆

The first official name of the Cincinnati ballclub was "The Resolutes" in the 1860s.

◆

The Cincinnati Reds joined the National League in 1890.

◆

The Cincinnati Reds beat the Philadelphia Phillies 2 to 1 in the first major league game played at night, on May 29, 1935.

◆

Rogers Hornsby managed the Cincinnati Reds in 1952 and 1953.

◆

Marge Schott was the owner of the Reds team that won the 1990 World Series. Lou Pinella was the manager of that team.

CLEVELAND INDIANS

◆

Cleveland has been an American League club since 1901. The team has several nicknames. At first, the club was called the Blues. It was also called the Bluebirds, the Broncos, and the Naps (after its famous manager). In 1915, the team became known as the Indians.

◆

Hall of Fame player Nap Lajoie was the Cleveland manager from 1905 to 1909.

◆

Addie Joss of the Cleveland Indians pitched a perfect game against the Chicago White Sox in 1908.

◆

Tris Speaker managed the Cleveland Indians to a World Series Championship in 1920.

On August 7, 2001, the Cleveland Indians overcame a 12-run deficit to the Seattle Mariners and came back to win the game 15 to 14 in historic fashion.

COLORADO ROCKIES

◆

The Colorado Rockies baseball team took the name of a pro hockey team that moved to New Jersey and became the Devils.

◆

Andres Galarraga was the first Colorado player to win a NL batting title, with a .370 average in 1993.

◆

Eric Young of the Rockies stole 53 bases in 1996, which was tops in the National League.

◆

Larry Walker of the Rockies led the National League with a .710 slugging percentage in 1999, and a .458 on base percentage.

DETROIT TIGERS

◆

Detroit has been in the American League since 1901 and has always been known as the Tigers.

◆

Ty Cobb was a player-manager of the Detroit Tigers from 1921 to 1926.

◆

Al Kaline played all of his 2,834 career games for the Tigers.

◆

Hank Greenberg smashed an American-League-leading 58 home runs for the Tigers in 1938.

FLORIDA MARLINS

◆

The Florida Marlins joined the National League in 1993.

◆

Chuck Carr of the Marlins led the National League with 58 stolen bases in 1993.

◆

In 1995, Gary Sheffield led all Marlins hitters with a .324 batting average.

◆

In 2000, Preston Wilson of the Marlins hit 31 home runs and stole 36 bases.

◆

Juan Pierre of the Marlins stole 65 bases in 2003. He also batted .305 that season.

◆

Jack McKeon was 72 years old when he managed the Marlins to the World Series championship in 2003.

HOUSTON ASTROS

◆

When Houston was granted a National League franchise in 1962, the team was originally named the Houston Colt 45s. Three years later, the team was renamed the Houston Astros.

◆

The Astros were the first major league ball team to play in an indoor park in 1965.

◆

The Astros beat the New York Mets 1 to 0 in 24 innings on August 23, 1989.

◆

Pitcher Andy Pettite of the Astros stuck out 10 Florida Marlins batters in seven innings in a game played on July 15, 2006.

KANSAS CITY ROYALS

◆

The Kansas City Royals joined the American League in 1969 as an expansion club.

◆

In 1979, Willie Wilson of the Kansas City Royals led the American League by stealing 83 bases.

◆

In 1980, the Kansas City Royals, managed by Jim Frey, lost to the Philadelphia Phillies managed by Dallas Green in the World Series.

◆

When the Kansas City Royals beat the St. Louis Cardinals to win the World Series Championship in 1985, Kansas City pitcher Bret Saberhagen was named the Most Valuable Player of the Series.

◆

Third baseman George Brett was voted the MVP of the American League Championship series in 1985.

LOS ANGELES DODGERS

◆

The Dodgers were known as the Brooklyn Bridgegrooms in 1888 and as the Brooklyn Trolley Dodgers from 1891 to 1898.

◆

The Brooklyn Dodgers moved from New York to California in 1958.

◆

Babe Ruth was a coach for the Brooklyn Dodgers in 1938.

◆

The Los Angeles Dodgers played 737 consecutive games without being rained out, until April 21, 1967. A second home rainout in April 1976 ended a streak of 724 straight games. From April 1988 to April 1999, the Dodgers played 856 home games without a rainout.

MILWAUKEE BREWERS

♦

The Seattle Pilots joined the American League in 1969. In 1970, the Pilots moved to Milwaukee and became the Brewers.

♦

In 1970, Tommy Harper of the Brewers hit 31 home runs and stole 38 bases.

♦

Harvey Kuenn managed the Brewers to the American League pennant in 1982.

♦

The Brewers left the American League to join the National League in 1998.

♦

Scott Podsednik led the Brewers with a .314 batting average in 2003. He also stole 43 bases.

♦

Richie Sexson of the Brewers hit 45 home runs in 2003.

MINNESOTA TWINS

♦

The Washington Senators moved to Minnesota in 1961 and became the Twins.

♦

Bob Allison and Harmon Killebrew of the Twins hit grand slams in the first inning of a game against the Cleveland Indians on July 18, 1962.

♦

The Twins won their first World Series in 1987 by beating the St. Louis Cardinals 4 games to 3.

♦

Manager Tom Kelly guided the Twins to World Series championships in 1987 and 1991.

♦

Ron Gardenshire managed the Minnesota Twins to division titles in his first three years in charge—2002 to 2004.

NEW YORK METS

The Mets moved to Shea Stadium in 1964. In the Mets' first two years of operation—1962 and 1963—they played their home games at New York's old Polo Grounds.

Willie Randolph got his first win as manager of the New York Mets on April 10, 2005.

Two New York Mets hit grand slams in the same game for the first time in history when Cliff Floyd and Carlos Beltran homered against the Chicago Cubs on July 16, 2006.

The Mets won their first World Series Championship in 1969, beating the Baltimore Orioles. They won their second National League Championship in 1973.

NEW YORK YANKEES

◆

The New York Yankees were originally called the New York Highlanders. The team name was changed to Yankees in their move to the Polo Grounds.

◆

The Yankees are sometimes called the Bronx Bombers.

◆

The Yankees won 19 consecutive games in 1947.

◆

David Cone of the Yankees pitched a perfect game against the Montreal Expos on Yogi Berra Day at Yankee Stadium on July 18, 1999.

◆

Pitcher Mariano Rivera earned the 400th save of his career on July 16, 2006 against the Chicago White Sox.

OAKLAND ATHLETICS

◆

The Oakland Athletics were known as the Philadelphia Athletics from 1901 to 1954. The team became the Kansas City A's in 1955. The A's played in Kansas City until 1967. Oakland became the Athletics' home in 1968.

◆

The Philadelphia Athletics, managed by Connie Mack, won World Series Championships in 1910, 1911, 1913, 1929, and 1930.

◆

The Oakland A's beat the Cincinnati Reds in the 1972 World Series four games to three games. Dick Williams was Oakland's manager in 1972. Catcher Gene Tenance of the Oakland A's was named the Most Valuable Player of the 1972 World Series.

◆

In 2005, Ken Macha was the manager of the Oakland Athletics.

PHILADELPHIA PHILLIES

The Philadelphia Phillies have been in the National League since 1883.

The Philadelphia Phillies won 16 consecutive games in 1887, 1890, 1892, and 1909.

On September 28, 1919, the Phillies played the New York Giants in a game that lasted 51 minutes. The Giants beat the Phillies 6 to 1.

In 1944 and 1945, the Phillies were known as the Philadelphia Blue Jays.

Jim Bunning of the Phillies pitched a perfect game against the New York Mets on June 21, 1964.

PITTSBURGH PIRATES

◆

The Pittsburgh Pirates entered the National League in 1887.

◆

The Pirates were called the Pittsburgh Alleghenies from 1887 to 1891.

◆

Roberto Clemente had 166 triples as a player for the Pittsburgh Pirates from 1955 to 1972.

◆

Paul Waner of the Pirates set a record by getting extra-base hits in 14 consecutive games in 1927.

◆

Manager Danny Murtaugh guided the Pittsburgh Pirates to a World Series championship in 1971.

SAN DIEGO PADRES

◆

Tony Gwynn of the San Diego Padres won eight NL batting titles.

◆

Don Zimmer managed the Padres in 1972 and 1973, his first major league assignments.

◆

Pitcher Gaylord Perry of the Padres was 30 years old when he won the Cy Young Award in 1978.

◆

Fred McGriff was the first San Diego player to win a NL home run title. McGriff belted 35 homers in 1992 to lead all National League sluggers.

◆

Trevor Hoffman of the Padres in 2004 became the second pitcher in major league history to achieve 400 career saves.

SAN FRANCISCO GIANTS

◆

In 1916, the New York Giants won 26 straight games.

◆

Bill Terry managed the New York Giants to a World Series championship in 1933.

◆

The New York Giants, managed by John McGraw, won back-to-back World Series championships in 1921 and 1922.

◆

The New York Giants moved to San Francisco for the 1958 NL season.

◆

Daryl Spencer was the first San Francisco Giant player to hit a home run in a National League game, against the Los Angeles Dodgers on opening day, April 15, 1958.

SEATTLE MARINERS

◆

The Seattle Mariners began play as an American League Club in 1977.

◆

In 1982, pitcher Bill Caudill of the Seattle Mariners was traded to the New York Yankees. Caudill's time in New York pinstripes was short lived. Twenty minutes later, the Yankees traded Bill to Seattle.

◆

In 2000 and 2001, the Mariners won the American League Division Series, but lost the Championship Series.

◆

Ichiro Suzuki of the Mariners set a Major League record with 262 hits in 2004.

ST. LOUIS CARDINALS

◆

The 1934 Cardinals team was known as "The Gashouse Gang" because of their rough style of play.

◆

Frankie Frisch struck out only 10 times as an every-day player for the Cardinals in 1927.

◆

Frankie Frisch managed the Cardinals to a World Series championship over the Detroit Tigers managed by Mickey Cochrane in 1934.

◆

Joe "Ducky" Medwick of the St. Louis Cardinals had 64 doubles in 1936, 56 doubles in 1937, and 47 doubles in 1938—all leading the National League.

TAMPA BAY DEVIL RAYS

The Tampa Bay Devil Rays joined the American League in 1998. They were almost called the Tampa Bay Manta Rays.

Fred McGriff was the top hitter for the Devil Rays in 1999. McGriff posted a .310 batting average that season.

Carl Crawford of the Devil Rays stole three bases against the Red Sox, including a steal of home on July 5, 2006. That season he reached 50 stolen bases for the third time in his career.

Pitcher Scott Kazmir of the Devil Rays was named to the 2006 American League All Star squad.

TEXAS RANGERS

◆

The Rangers were an expansion team in 1961 and were originally the Washington Senators. In 1972, the team moved to Texas and changed its name.

◆

On June 4, 1974, the Texas Rangers won a forfeit game from the Cleveland Indians when umpire Nestor Chylak had continual trouble with unruly Indian's fans in Cleveland.

◆

Pitcher Nolan Ryan of the Rangers led the American League in strikeouts in 1989 and 1990. Ryan fanned 301 batters in 1989 and 232 in 1990.

◆

Buck Showalter was the manager of the Texas Rangers in 2005.

TORONTO BLUE JAYS

◆

Toronto became known as the Blue Jays thanks to a "Name the Team" contest held in 1976.

◆

The Toronto Blue Jays played in the American League for the first time in 1977.
In 1985, Bobby Cox of the Toronto Blue Jays was the American League manager of the year.

◆

The Toronto Blue Jays won World Series Championships in 1992 and 1993. In 1992, Toronto beat the Atlanta Braves four games to two games in the World Series. In 1993, the Blue Jays beat the Philadelphia Phillies four games to two games to win the World championship.

◆

Pitcher Roger Clemens of the Toronto Blue Jays led the AL in strikeouts in 1997 and 1998.

WASHINGTON NATIONALS

◆

The Washington Nationals were originally the Montreal Expos, who joined the National League in 1969.

◆

In 1971, Ron Hunt of the Montreal Expos was hit a major-league-record 50 times. He led the National League in getting hit by pitches in his last seven seasons.

◆

Ron LeFlore of Montreal was the first Expos player to lead the National League in stolen bases, with 97 in 1980.

◆

Tim Raines of the Montreal Expos won the National League batting crown in 1986 with a .334 average. Raines was the first Montreal (now Washington) player to win a batting title.

CHAPTER 12
Pennants, All-Stars & The World Series

I n baseball, the goal is to be the best. Teams want to be the best in their league. Players want to be the best at their position. Pennant winners and All-Star players want to be World Series Champions.

This chapter is all about the best of the best in baseball.

◆

Baseball's first All-Star game was played on July 6, 1933, at Chicago's Comiskey Park. The American League All-Stars won that game 4 to 2.

◆

Ryan Howard of the Philadelphia Phillies was the Home Run Derby Champion of the 2006 baseball All-Star game.

Babe Ruth of the New York Yankees smashed the first home run ever hit in an All-Star contest. Babe belted a two run blast in the third inning of the 1933 All-Star game.

◆

Derrek Lee of the Chicago Cubs was named to the All-Star game for the first time in 2005.

◆

Carlton Fisk of the Boston Red Sox won Game Six of the 1975 World Series against the Cincinnati Reds by hitting a home run in the bottom of the 12th inning. However, the Reds eventually won the 1975 Championship, beating the Red Sox four games to three.

◆

Reggie Jackson of the New York Yankees hit three home runs in Game Six of the 1977 World Series against the Los Angeles Dodgers. The Yankees won the 1977 World Championship, and Jackson was named the Most Valuable Player of the Series.

Six New York Mets players were named to the 2006 All-Star team. The players honored were third baseman David Wright, shortstop Jose Reyes, catcher Paul LoDuca, pitcher Pedro Martinez, outfielder Carlos Beltran, and pitcher Tom Glavine.

◆

Frankie Frisch of the St. Louis Cardinals was the first National League player to hit a home run in an All-Star contest. Frisch clubbed a homer in the sixth inning of the 1933 All-Star Classic.

◆

In 1940, the Detroit Tigers won the American League pennant by finishing one game ahead of the Cleveland Indians and two games ahead of the New York Yankees.

◆

The American League defeated the National League three to two in the 2006 All-Star game.

Yogi Berra played in 75 World Series games. Berra pounded out 71 World Series hits and blasted 12 World Series home runs.

◆

Don Larsen of the New York Yankees was named the MVP of the 1956 World Series that season.

◆

Chase Utley of the Philadelphia Phillies was the starting second baseman for the National League in the 2006 All-Star game.

◆

In 1956, the Brooklyn Dodgers won the National League pennant by finishing one game ahead of the Milwaukee Braves and two games ahead of the Cincinnati Reds.

Roberto Clemente of the Pittsburgh Pirates was the Most Valuable Player of the 1971 World Series.

◆

Jason Bay of the Pittsburgh Pirates was a starting outfielder for the National League in the 2006 All-Star game.

◆

Pepper Martin of the St. Louis Cardinals had a career batting average of .418 in World Series play.

◆

Paul Molitor of the Milwaukee Brewers and the Toronto Blue Jays batted .418 in 55 World Series at bats.

◆

The 1961 baseball All-Star game was halted because of rain and officially declared a tie.

◆

Pitcher Sandy Koufax of the Los Angeles Dodgers was the Most Valuable Player of the 1963 World Series and the 1965 World Series.

The American League All-Stars beat the National League All-Stars 7 to 5 in the 2005 All-Star game. Phil Garner, who managed the Houston Astros to the National League pennant in 2005, was a player on the Pittsburgh Pirates team that won the 1979 World Series.

◆

Marquis Grissom had a career batting average of .390 in World Series competition. Grissom collected 30 hits in 77 at bats in the World Series.

◆

In 1987, it took thirteen innings to decide a winner of baseball's All-Star game. The National League beat the American League 2 to 0 in extra innings.

St. Louis Cardinals shortstop Edgar Renteria made the final out of the 2004 World Series won by the Boston Red Sox. Renteria grounded to pitcher Keith Foulke, who threw to first baseman Doug Mientkiewicz to record the out.

◆

Mickey Mantle scored 42 runs in World Series competition.

◆

New York Yankees slugger Mickey Mantle hit 18 home runs in World Series play.

◆

Mickey Mantle had 40 RBIs while playing in 65 World Series games.

◆

Whitey Ford of the New York Yankees pitched in 22 World Series games and had a career series record of 10 wins and 8 losses. Ford also struck out 94 batters in World Series play.

David Ortiz of the Boston Red Sox was the starting first baseman for the American League in the 2006 All-Star game. Ortiz's teammate Mark Loretta was the starting second baseman on the AL squad.

◆

Bucky Harris of the Washington Senators was the first American League player to hit safely in all seven games of a World Series. In 1924, Harris hammered out hits in all seven games of the series against the New York Giants to lead the Senators to a world championship. Bucky Harris was Washington's player/manager and had 11 hits in 33 at bats for a .333 average.

◆

Charles "Chief" Bender of the Philadelphia Athletics pitched in ten World Series games and had a career record of six wins and four losses.

The 2002 All-Star game was halted by Baseball Commissioner Bud Selig with the score tied at seven all in the 11th inning. Selig stopped the contest because neither the American League nor the National League had any pitchers left to use. There was no MVP named in the contest.

◆

Derek Jeter of the New York Yankees was the starting shortstop for the American League in the 2006 All-Star game. Jeter's teammate Alex Rodriguez was the starting third baseman for the American League All-Stars.

◆

David Eckstein of the St. Louis Cardinals was the starting shortstop for the National League in the 2005 All-Star game.

◆

Mark Sweeney of the San Diego Padres made the final out of the 1998 World Series. Sweeney grounded to New York. Yankees' third baseman

Scott Brosius. Brosius threw to Tino Martinez, the first baseman, who recorded the out. The Yankees won the Championship in four games.

◆

Pitcher Mike Hampton of the New York Mets was the Most Valuable Player of the National League Championship series in 2000.

◆

Dave Robertson of the New York Giants hit safely in all six games of the 1917 World Series against the Chicago White Sox. Robertson collected 11 hits in 22 at bats for a .500 batting average in the Series. The White Sox, however, won the Championship four games to two games.

◆

The St. Louis Cardinals beat the Detroit Tigers 4 games to 3 in the 1934 World Series. The four Cardinals pitching victories were recorded by Dizzy Dean and his brother Daffy Dean. Dizzy Dean won Games One and Seven of the Series. Daffy Dean won Games Three and Six of the 1934 World Series.

◆

The Chicago White Sox beat the Boston Red Sox three games to none in the 2005 ALCS. The Red Sox were the defending World Champions at the time. The White Sox went on to win the 2005 World Series.

◆

Jeff Kent of the Los Angeles Dodgers was the starting second baseman for the National League in the 2005 All-Star game.

◆

Lew Burdette won three games against the New York Yankees while pitching for the Milwaukee Braves in the 1957 World Series. The Braves won the Championship in 1957, beating the Yankees four games to three games.

Pitcher Darold Knowles of the Oakland A's appeared in all seven games of the 1973 World Series against the New York Mets. Oakland won the 1973 World Championship, beating New York 4 games to 3 games.

◆

Shortstop Larry Brown of the Philadelphia Phillies helped turn seven double plays against the Kansas City Royals in the 1980 World Series.

◆

The Philadelphia Phillies, managed by Dallas Green, won the 1980 World Series. Third baseman Mike Schmidt of Philadelphia was the Most Valuable Player of the Series.

◆

Cito Gaston managed the Toronto Blue Jays to World Series Championships in 1992 and 1993.

The first National League victory in the All-Star game came in 1936 when the NL All-Stars beat the AL All-Stars 4 to 1.

♦

In 1969, first baseman Donn Clendenon of the New York Mets was named the Most Valuable Player of the World Series.

♦

Alfonso Soriano was the MVP of the 2004 All-Star game as a second baseman. Soriano was an All-Star pick at second base again in 2005. Alfonso Soriano made the 2006 All-Star team as an outfielder.

♦

David Justice of the New York Yankees was the Most Valuable Player of the American League Championship Series in 2000.

♦

Pitcher Bob Gibson of the St. Louis Cardinals struck out 92 batters in World Series competition.

Outfielder Vladimir Guerrero of the Anaheim Angels was a member of the American League All-Star team in 2005 and 2006.

◆

Pitcher Oral Hershiser of the Cleveland Indians was the Most Valuable Player of the ACLS in 1995.

◆

While playing for the Los Angeles Dodgers pitcher Oral Hershiser was the MVP of the National League Championship Series in 1988.

◆

On October 9, 1916, the Boston Red Sox and the Brooklyn Dodgers played a 14-inning World Series game. Boston beat the Dodgers 2 to 1 in the contest, which was the second game of the Series. The winning pitcher for Boston was Babe Ruth. The Red sox also won the Championship 4 games to 1 game.

Bob Brenly managed the Arizona Diamondbacks to a World Series championship in 2001.

◆

Pitcher Josh Beckett of the Florida Marlins was the Most Valuable Player of the 2003 World Series.

◆

In 1983, the American League beat the National League 13 to 3 in baseball's All-Star game.

◆

In 1991, pitcher Steve Avery of the Atlanta Braves was the MVP of the National League Championship series. Pitcher John Smoltz of the Atlanta Braves was the Most Valuable Player of the NLCS in 1992.

◆

Lou Brock of the St. Louis Cardinals stole 14 bases in 21 World Series games.

Christy Mathewson of the New York Giants pitched 27 scoreless innings against the Philadelphia Athletics in the 1905 World Series.

◆

Bo Jackson of the Kansas City Royals was the Most Valuable Player of the 1989 All-Star game.

◆

The New York Yankees beat the Pittsburgh Pirates 12 to 0 in the sixth game of the 1960 World Series.

◆

Davey Johnson managed the New York Mets to a World Series Championship in 1986.

◆

The Pittsburgh Pirates lost only 36 games when they won the National League pennant in 1902. Pittsburgh finished the regular season with a record of 103 wins and 36 losses.

When the Chicago Cubs won the NL pennant in 1906, they lost only 36 games. Chicago won 116 games and lost 36 games in 1906.

◆

Bobby Cox managed the Atlanta Braves to the World Series crown in 1995.

◆

Johnny Callison of the Philadelphia Phillies was the Most Valuable Player of the 1964 All-Star game.

◆

Jeff Conine of the Florida Marlins was the MVP of the 1995 All-Star game.

Shortstop Michael Young of the Texas Rangers was the Most Valuable Player of Major League Baseball's 2006 All-Star game.

◆

Will Clark of the San Francisco Giants was the MVP of the National League Championship Series in 1989.

◆

Hank Aaron had a .364 career batting average in World Series play.

◆

Christy Mathewson of the New York Giants pitched 11 complete World Series games during his career.

◆

The Cincinnati Reds won the National League pennant for the first time in 1919 when they finished with a season record of 96 wins and 44 losses.

CHAPTER 13
Touching All the Bases

It's time to tally up the box score, baseball buffs before we exit the ball park. It's time to touch all of the bases when it comes to diamond data. In this chapter, you'll learn that baseball can be a sport enjoyed by the entire family generation after generation. You'll also glean interesting bits and pieces of baseball facts and information from one-hit wonders to all time team players. The umpire is ready to start, so step up to the plate and swing for the fences.

It's time to touch them all.

Shin-soo Choo hit his first career home run in his debut for the Cleveland Indians on July 28, 2006. Choo's homer gave Cleveland a 1 to 0 victory over the Seattle Mariners.

◆

In 2006, Effa Manley became the first woman elected to the Baseball Hall of Fame. Manley was an owner of the Newark Eagles, a Negro league baseball team, in the 1940s.

◆

David Wright of the New York Mets hit a home run in his first at bat during his first All-Star game appearance. It happened in 2006.

◆

The Cincinnati Reds and the Pittsburgh Pirates played the last triple header in Major League baseball on October 2, 1920.

Jack Graney, who retired in 1921 as a player for the Cleveland Indians, is believed to be the first former pro baseball player to become a sports announcer. Graney was the Indians' play by play announcer from 1933 to 1954.

◆

The New York Yankees played 156 games in 1932 and were not shut out a single time.

◆

Chuck Tanner of the Mikwaukee Braves hit a home run on the first pitch thrown to him as a major lea-guer on April 12, 1955.

◆

Branch Rickey, the famous owner of the Brooklyn Dodgers, was cut from the Cincinnati Reds in the early 1900s for refusing to play baseball games on Sundays. Rickey had promised his mother he wouldn't play Sunday games when he turned pro. Branch Rickey later played for the St. Louis Browns and the New York Highlanders.

George Steinbrenner, the owner of the New York Yankees, is a real Yankee Doodle Dandy. His birthday is July 4.

◆

Catcher Mike Piazza of the San Diego Padres got the 2,000th hit of his career against the San Francisco Giants on July 21, 2006. The hit was a double.

◆

Bobo Newsom was traded 17 times during his 20-year major league career.

◆

Alex Rodriguez of the New York Yankees got his 200th career hit on July 21, 2006 against the Toronto Blue Jays. Rodriguez' hit was a home run. It was also the 450th homer of A-Rod's career.

◆

Sophie Kurys of the All American Girls Professional Baseball League stole 201 bases in 203 attempts in 1946.

In 1912, pitcher Rube Marquard of the New York Giants won 19 consecutive games.

◆

Johnny Mize, of the St. Louis Cardinals and the New York Giants, hit three homers in a single game six times during his career.

◆

Jim Hickman was the first New York Mets player to hit for the cycle. He did it on August 7, 1963.

◆

Hank Aaron, one of baseball's greatest hitters, got his first chance to play in the major leagues when the Braves' Bobby Thompson broke his ankle in spring training.

◆

Duke Snider of the Brooklyn Dodgers hit four home runs in a single World Series game in 1952 and again in 1955. Snider did it against the New York Yankees both times.

Pitcher Carl Erskine of the Brooklyn Dodgers
whiffed 14 New York Yankee batters in a 1953
World Series game.

◆

Carroll Hardy was the only player to ever pinch hit
for both Ted Williams and Carl Yastrzemski. Hardy
pinch hit for Williams in 1960 and for Yastrzemski
in 1961.

Brothers Mort and Walker Cooper played for the St. Louis Cardinals in 1944 when the Cardinals beat the St. Louis Browns to win the World Series.

◆

Brothers Mack and Zack Wheat combined for over 3,000 hits during their major league careers.

◆

Brothers Joe, Luke, and Tom Sewell all played major league baseball.

◆

Honus Wagner was a baseball Hall of Famer. Honus' brother, Butts Wagner also played major league baseball.

◆

Brothers Joe, Dom, and Vince DiMaggio were all major league baseball players.

◆

Brothers Ed, Frank, Jim, Joe, and Tom Delahanty all played professional baseball.

Eduardo Perez of the Tampa Bay Devil Rays is the son of baseball Hall of Famer Tony Perez.

◆

Ray Boone was a major league player for several major league teams. His son, Bob Boone, also played for numerous major league clubs. Bob Boone's sons Aaron Boone and Bret Boone also played Major League baseball.

◆

Tito Francona played outfield and first base in the major leagues. Tito's son, Terry Francona, also played outfield in the major leagues. Terry Francona went on to manage the Boston Red Sox to a World Series championship.

◆

Manny Mota starred for the San Francisco Giants and other teams. Manny's sons, Andy Mota and Jose Mota, played for the Houston Astros and the San Diego Padres respectively.

Cal Ripkin, Sr. never appeared in a major league game. He was a minor league catcher. However, he was a major league coach. His sons, Cal Ripkin, Jr., and Billy Ripkin were both major league players.

◆

Pitcher Roger Clemens son Koby was drafted by the Houston Astros.

◆

Major League baseball star, Bobby Bonds, is the father of major league baseball star Barry Bonds.

Former Major League player Sandy Alomar is the father of major league players Roberto Alomar and Sandy Alomar, Jr.

◆

Yogi Berra and his son, Dale Berra, both played major league baseball.

CHAPTER 14
The Last Inning

Dale Berra was once asked to compare his baseball skills to those of his Hall-of-Fame father. Dale Berra responded, "Our similarities are different."

It's amazing how many Hollywood stars, famous folks, and celebrities once dreamed or aspired to be pro baseball players. Some came close to attaining their goal. Others failed as pro athletes and gained fame in other areas like movies, politics, and acting. The fame game of baseball has a long and interesting history. So, read on and check out this list of former baseball famous folks.

◆

United States President George H.W. Bush played baseball in college.

President George Bush was an owner of the Texas Rangers baseball club.

◆

Academy Award-winning actor Richard Widmark's daughter Ann was Hall of Fame pitcher Sandy Koufax's first wife.

◆

Movie actor Chuck Connors, who starred as the Rifleman in the famous T.V. western show, was a pitcher for the Los Angeles Dodgers organization.

◆

Actor Paul Gleason, who starred as the vice principal in the movie *The Breakfast Club*, played Triple A minor league baseball in the 1950s.

◆

Hall of Fame pitcher Don Drysdale of the Los Angeles Dodgers often appeared as a guest star on the old *Donna Reed* T.V. Show.

◆

Keith Hernandez, who won the NL batting title in 1979, guest-starred on the T.V. show *Seinfeld*.

◆

The film *The Pride of the Yankees*, starring Gary Cooper, was a movie about the life story of New York Yankee Lou Gehrig. In the film, the part of Babe Ruth was played by Babe Ruth.

◆

The movie *The Jackie Robinson Story* starred Jackie Robinson as himself. It also starred actress Ruby Dee.

◆

Actor and United States President Ronald Reagan played Hall of Fame pitcher Grover Cleveland Alexander in the movie *The Winning Team*.

◆

The movie *The Pride of St. Louis*, starring Dan Dailey and Joanne Dru, is about the life story of Hall of Fame pitcher Dizzy Dean.

The movie *Fear Strikes Out* is about the life story of Boston Red Sox outfielder Jimmy Piersall.

◆

The movie *Bang the Drum Slowly* featured a young Robert DeNiro as a major league catcher who was fatally ill. It was based on the novel by Mark Harris.

◆

Comic Richard Pryor starred as an aspiring major league pitcher in the movie *Brewster's Millions*.

◆

Kevin Costner, Tim Robbins, and Charlie Sheen starred in the hit baseball movie *Bull Durham*.

◆

Businessman Donald Trump was a catcher and first baseman who was the captain of the baseball team at New York Military Academy.

Former Secretary of Homeland Security, Tom Ridge, tried out for his high school baseball team.

◆

The movie *Eight Men Out* is about the 1919 Chicago Back Sox Scandal. It is about Chicago White Sox players being bribed to throw the World Series. The movie is based on the book of the same name by Eliot Asinof.

◆

Television commentator Bill O'Reilly was a pitcher on his high school baseball team.

◆

The Natural, starring Robert Redford as fictional baseball star Roy Hobbs, is one of the best sports stories ever made. It is based on the novel by Bernard Malamud.

◆

The Bad News Bears is a comedy about Little League baseball starring Walter Matthau and Tatum O'Neal.

⭐ INDEX ⭐

Aaron, Henry, 62, 127, 232, 249, 251, 273, 277, 322, 327

AB, definition of, 77

Abbott, Jim, 152, 275

Abreau, Bobby, 132

Adams, John Quincy, 89

Adcock, Joe, 254

Agee, Tommie, 145, 244

Alexander, Grover Cleveland, 155, 174, 176, 335

Alfonzo, Edgardo, 109

Alfonzo, Eliezer, 194

All-American Girls Professional Baseball League founding of, 40, 180 original team members of, 42 year it folded, 44

Allen, Dick, 270

Allison, Bob, 291

Alomar, Roberto, 332

Alomar, Sandy, Jr., 183, 332

Alou, Felipe, 97, 133

Alou, Matty, 133

Alou, Moises, 133

Altobelli, Joe, 278

American League Central Division, 42 East Division, 38 first president of, 26 West Division, 43

American Legion baseball, 25

Anaheim Angels, 275

Anderson, Garrett, 144

Anderson, Sparky, 35, 108, 198, 199

Ankiel, Rick, 128

Appling, Luke, 220

Arizona Diamondbacks 15, 276, 319

"Around the horn," definition of, 75

Ashburn, Richie, 100, 145

Ashford, Emmett, 9

Asinof, Eliot, 337

Atlanta Braves, 277, 321

Avery, Steve, 319

Ayala, Benny, 264

Bad New Bears, The, 337

Baerga, Carlos, 19, 276

Bagby, Jim, 163

Bagwell, Jeff, 100, 145, 266

Baker, Dusty, 199

Baker, Frank "Home Run," 50

Baltimore Orioles, 278

Bang the Drum Slowly, 336

"Banjo hit," definition of, 76

Banks, Ernie, 118, 247, 259, 263

Barker, Len, 157

Barrow, Ed, 67

Baseball cards, 34

Baseball, description of, 83

Baseball game, first organized, 47

Base to base distance, 74

"Bat boy," definition of, 86

Bat Day, first, 38

"Batter's box," description of, 78

"Battery," definition of, 71

"Batting average," definition of, 77

Batting helmets, required use of, 36

Batting order, definition of, 78

"Batting stance," definition of, 78

Bay, Jason, 308

"BB," definition of, 71

"Bean ball," definition of, 71

Beckett, Josh, 319

Bell, Buddy, 110

Bell, David, 110

Bell, Gus, 110, 227

Belle, Albert, 238

Beltran, Carlos, 132, 292, 307

Bench, Johnny, 14, 194, 246, 266

Bender, Charles "Chief," 312

Benson, Kris, 161

Benton, Al, 178

Berkman, Lance, 144

Berra, Dale, 332, 333

Berra, Yogi, 44, 47, 187, 193, 195, 196, 209, 237, 248, 308, 332, 333

Bichette, Dante, 267

Biggio, Craig, 56, 100, 109

Black Sox scandal, 53–55

"Blooper," definition of, 76

Blue, Vida, 156

Blyleven, Bert, 158

Boggs, Wade, 111, 235

Bonds, Barry, 28, 46, 145, 216, 217, 252, 271, 331

Bonds, Bobby, 264, 266, 331

Boone, Aaron, 271, 330

Boone, Bob, 330

Boone, Bret, 105, 236, 330

Boone, Ray, 330

Borden, Joe, 12

Boros, Steve, 212

Boston Braves, 60

Boston Red Sox, 9, 40, 279, 280, 318

Bouncing ball call, 72, 84

Bowa, Larry, 206

Boyer, "Clete," 113

Branca, Ralph, 257

Breakfast Club, The, 334

Brenly, Bob, 319

Brett, George, 231, 288

Brewster's Millions, 336

Bristol, Dave, 209

Britton, Helen, 10

Brock, Lou, 139, 232, 319

Brodie, Ping, 248

Bronx Bombers, 293

Brooklyn Bridegrooms, 18

Brooklyn Dodgers, 17, 308, 318

Brown, Bobby, 115

Brown, Ike, 30

Brown, Larry, 316

Brucker, Victoria, 29

Buckner, Bill, 97, 245

Bulkeley, Morgan G., 26

Bull Durham, 336

Bullpen, definition of, 71

Bunning, Jim, 163, 295

"Bunt," definition of, 83

Burdette, Lew, 154, 315

Burgess, Smokey, 240

Burns, George, 99

Busch Stadium, 12

Bush, George, 334

Bush, George H.W., 333

Butler, Brett, 144

Cabrera, Miguel, 134

Cairo, Miguel, 124

Callison, Johnny, 321

Campanella, Roy, 182, 260

"Can of corn," definition of, 76

Carew, Rod, 105, 230, 247

Carlton, Steve, 12, 158, 162, 176

Carr, Chuck, 286

Carter, Gary, 187

Cartwright, Alexander, 38

Carty, Rico, 219

Castillo, Luis, 102

Castro, Fidel, 180

Catcher's mask, first, 9

Catchers, 181–196

Catching firsts, 14

Caudill, Bill, 299

"Caught looking," definition of, 82

Centerfielder, description of, 136

Cepeda, Orlando, 92, 94, 95

Cey, Ron, 113

Chambliss, Chris, 97

Chance, Dean, 16, 177

Chance, Frank, 92, 203

Chandler, Spud, 116, 117

"Changeup," definition of, 31

Chapman, Ray, 121

"Chatter," definition of, 73

Chesbro, Jack, 51

Chest protector, first time won, 14

Chicago Black Sox Scandal, 53, 54, 55, 337

Chicago Cubs, 59, 280, 321

Chicago White Sox, 16, 24, 53, 54, 281, 315

Chicago White Stockings, 40

"Choke up," definition of, 78

Choo, Shin-soo, 324

Chylak, Nestor, 302

Cicotte, Eddie, 53, 54

Cincinnati Reds, 282, 322, 324

Cincinnati Red Stockings, 11

"Circus catch," definition of, 87

Clark, Will, 99, 322

"Cleanup hitter," definition of, 78

Clemens, Koby, 331

Clemens, Roger, 148, 303, 331

Clemente, Roberto, 127, 128, 136, 220, 296, 308

Clemson, 60

Clendenon, Donn, 317

Cleveland Indians, 19, 283, 284

Cleveland Spiders, 56

Cloninger, Tony, 33

Cobb, Ty, 35, 58, 60, 139, 146, 222, 233, 241, 268, 285

Cochrane, Mickey, 193, 300

Colavito, Rocky, 141, 265

Colbert, Nate, 268

Coleman, Choo Choo, 192

College baseball game, first, 67

Collins, Eddie, 53, 234

Colon, Bartolo, 16, 151

Colorado Rockies, 27, 284

Combs, Earle, 228

Comiskey, Charles, 54

Comiskey Park, 25, 281, 305

Concepcion, Dave, 121

Cone, David, 154, 293

Conigliaro, Tony, 144

Conine, Jeff, 321

Connors, Chuck, 334

Conseco, Jose, 140, 271

Cooper, Gary, 335

Cooper, Mort, 329

Cooper, Walker, 329

Costner, Kevin, 336

Counsell, Craig, 102

Cox, Bobby, 61, 203, 212, 303, 321

Crawford, Carl, 128, 301

Crawford, Sam, 242

Crisp, Coco, 130

Crosby, Bobby, 119

Cummings, Arthur "Candy," 21

Curthright, Guy, 281

Dahlen, Bill, 280

Dailey, Dan, 335

Damon, Johnny, 126

Davis, George, 21

Davis, Mark, 173

Davis, Tommy, 225

Davis, Willie, 134

Dawson, Andre, 225

Dean, Daffy, 314, 315

Dean, Dizzy, 165, 167, 314, 315, 335

Dee, Ruby, 335

Delahanty brothers, 329

Delahanty, Ed, 20

Delgado, Carlos, 11, 46, 92

DeNiro, Robert, 336

Dent, Bucky, 121, 263

Designated hitter rule, 86

Detroit Tigers, 285, 307

"Diamond," definition of, 72

Dickey, Bill, 183, 193, 247

DiMaggio, Dom, 216, 329

DiMaggio, Joe, 15, 58, 61, 138, 141, 227, 273, 329

DiMaggio, Vince, 329

"Dinger," definition of, 80

Doby, Larry, 262

Donna Reed, 334

Donut weight, origins of, 78

Doubleday, Abner, 67

"Double," definition of, 85

"Doubleheader," definition of, 77

"Double play,"
definition of, 87
"Double steal,"
definition of, 77
Drogo, Walt, 22, 23
Dru, Joanne, 335
Drysdale, Don, 177,
180, 269, 334
Duffy, Hugh, 225
Dugleby, William, 63
Durocher, Leo," 203,
208
Dye, Jermaine, 60
Dykstra, Lenny, 143
Easley, Damion, 253
Eckersley, Dennis,
148
Eckstein, David,
119, 313
Edmonds, Jim, 128
Egyptian batting
contests, 41
Ehmke, Howard,
153
Eight Men Out, 337
"Error," definition of,
75
Erskine, Carl, 168,
328
Fair ball rule, 50
Fantasy baseball
leagues, first, 19

"Farm team,"
definition of, 87
Fear Strikes Out, 336
Feller, Bob, 173, 177
Felsch, Oscar
"Happy," 53, 54
Fenway Park, 26
Fidrych, Mark, 175
Fielder, Cecil, 245
Fielder, definition of,
75
Fingers, Rollie, 156
First basemen, 89–90
First College Baseball
Series, 22, 23
First night game, 25,
33, 36
Fisk, Carlton, 183,
186, 306
Fitzsimmons,
Freddie, 179
Five-sided home
plate, 76
"Flare," definition of,
76
Florida Marlins, 13,
286
Floyd, Cliff, 11, 292
Ford, Whitey, 173,
311
Forsch, Bob, 162
Forsch, Ken, 162

Foster, George, 139,
239, 270
Foul ball rule, 47, 52
Foul tips, and strikes,
71
400 batting average,
221–228
Four strike rule, 50
Fox, Jimmie, 228
Fox, Nellie, 104
Foxx, Jimmie, 64,
98, 226, 245, 249,
272, 273
Franco, John, 155, 175
Franco, Julio, 65, 102
Francona, Terry, 207,
330
Francona, Tito, 330
Frederick, Johnny,
219
Frey, Jim, 288
Friend, Bob, 31
Frisch, Frankie, 300,
307
Gagne, Eric, 152
Galarraga, Andres,
98, 284
Gandil, Arnold
"Chick," 53, 54
Garagiola, Joe, 47, 192
Garciaparra, Nomar,
35, 224

Gardenshire, Ron, 291

Garner, Phil, 310

Garvey, Steve, 94, 95, 253

"Gashouse Gang, The," 300

Gaston, Cito, 316

Gehrig, Lou, 48, 58, 59, 90, 120, 219, 237, 273, 335

Gehringer, Charlie, 116, 117

"Georgia Peach, The," 58

Georgia Tech, 61

Giambi, Jason, 98

Gibson, Bob, 155, 176, 317

Gibson, Josh, 186

Giles, Marcus, 109

Giraldi, Joe, 207

Glavine, Tom, 161, 307

Gleason, Paul, 334

Gomez, Vernon "Lefty," 179, 163, 249

Gonzalez, Luis, 134, 276

Gooden, Dwight, 170, 171

Gordon, Joe, 108

Graney, Jack, 325

Gray, Dolly, 166

Gray, Pete, 141

Green, Dallas, 288

Green, Shawn, 248

Greenberg, Hank, 218, 285

Greene, Khalil, 60

Griffey Jr., Ken, 131, 143, 262, 265

Grissom, Marquis, 310

Grove, Lefty, 174, 176

Gruber, Harry, 169

Guerrero, Pedro, 113

Guerrero, Vladimir, 136, 145, 318

Guidry, Ron, 157, 175

Guillen, Ozzie, 207

Gwen, Mickey, 187

Gwynn, Tony, 132, 215, 218, 230, 246, 297

Hafner, Travis, 251

Haller, Bill, 10

Haller, Tom, 10

Hampton, Mike, 314

Hardy, Carroll, 328

Hargrave, Bubbles, 215

Harper, Tommy, 290

Harris, Bucky, 202, 312

Harris, Mark, 336

Harrison, Benjamin, 25

Hartnett, Gabby, 193

Heilmann, Harry, 135, 216, 221

Helton, Todd, 100, 171, 217

Henderson, Ricky, 269

Henrich, Joe, 141

Herman, Babe, 244, 246, 246

Herman, Billy, 179

Hermida, Jeremy, 36

Hernandez, Keith, 90, 96, 335

Hernandez, Ramon, 194

Hershiser, Oral, 318

Hickman, Jim, 327

Hidalgo, Richard, 134

Higgins, Mike, 22, 23

"High cheese," definition of, 69

"Hitting for the cycle," definition of, 79

Hoag, Myril, 224

Hodges, Gil, 93, 264, 273
Hodges, Russ, 257
Hoffman, Trevor, 297
Hollomon, Alva "Bobo," 21, 171
Holtzman, Ken, 168
Hornsby, Rogers, 51, 103, 222, 223, 242, 282
"Hot corner," definition of, 82
Houk, Ralph, 202
Houston Astros, 287
Howard, Elston, 28, 78, 187
Howard, Frank, 93, 262, 266
Howard, Ryan, 98, 305
Hubbell, Carl, 169, 171
Huggins, Miller, 81, 211
Hundley, Todd, 191
Hunt, Ron, 45, 304
Hunter, Jim "Catfish," 168
Infield fly rule, 28
International Association, organization of, 67

"Iron Horse, The," 58
Jackie Robinson Story, The, 335
Jackson, Bo, 320
Jackson, Joe, 223, 281
Jackson, Reggie, 141, 258, 261, 306
Jackson, "Shoeless" Joe, 53, 54
Jacobs, Mike, 96
Jay, Joey, 277
Jenkins, Ferguson, 160
Jeter, Derek, 9, 120, 237, 313
Jethroe, Sam, 60
Johjima, Kenji, 20
Johnson, Alex, 228
Johnson, Davey, 320
Johnson, Howard, 267
Johnson, Randy, 157, 159, 276
Johnson, Walter R., 49, 151, 159, 169, 177, 248
Jones, Chipper, 22, 23, 114, 126, 277
Jones, Cleon, 227
Joss, Addie, 283
Justice, David, 317

K, in baseball scorebook, 70
Kaat, Jim, 150
Kaline, Al, 230, 285
Kamenshek, Dottie, 215
Kamieniecki, Scott, 275
Kansas City Monarchs, 13
Kansas City Royals, 25, 288
Kazmir, Scott, 301
Keeler, "Wee" Willie, 238, 248
Keller, Charley, 141
Kelly, Tom, 291
Kennedy, Adam, 103
Kent, Jeff, 315
Kerr, Dickie, 53
Killebrew, Harmon, 89, 94, 95, 269, 291
"Killer," 94, 95
"Killer B's," 100
Kilroy, Matt, 45
Kiner, Ralph, 24, 81, 137, 180, 264, 267, 273
Kingman, Dave, 145, 270
Klein, Chuck, 225, 245
Kluszewski, Ted, 224

Knowles, Darold, 316

"Knuckleball," definition of, 31

Konstanty, Jim, 165

Koosman, Jerry, 155

Koufax, Sandy, 51, 166, 172, 177, 200, 309, 334

Kuenn, Harvey, 290

Kurys, Sophie, 326

Lajoie, Nap, 57, 217, 222, 283

Landis, Kenesaw Mountain, 26, 55

Langston, Mark, 167

Larsen, Don, 64, 170, 308

LaRussa, Tony, 199, 202

"Laser," definition of, 82

Lasorda, Tommy, 184, 204, 208

Lavagetto, Cookie, 213

Lazzeri, Tony, 260

Lee, Derek, 92, 306

LeFlore, Ron, 142, 304

Leiter, Al, 13

Lemmon, Bob, 208

Lidge, Brad, 35

Lis, Joe, 97

Little League
  baseball game, distance from base to base, 74
  baseball game, innings, 73
  first baseball game, 16
  and Dontrelle Wilis, 153
  first female to play in World Series, 29
  first female starting pitcher in World Series, 24
  first female umpire in World Series, 31
  and girls participation, 18
  and pitcher's rubber, 71

Lloyd, Waner, 138

LoDuca, Paul, 191, 307

Logan, Johnny, 122

Lolich, Mickey, 148

Lombardi, Ernie, 190

Long, Dale, 268

Lopez, Al, 206, 207

Lopez, Javy, 182

Loretta, Mark, 312

Los Angeles Angels, 16

Los Angeles Dodgers, 220, 288

Luzinski, Greg, 244

Lyle, Sparky, 151, 163

Macha, Ken, 294

Mack, Connie, 14, 25, 60, 198, 294

Maddux, Greg, 151

Mahler, Rich, 149

Malamud, Bernand, 337

Managers, 197–213

Manley, Effa, 324

Mantle, Mickey, 12, 118, 135, 138, 215, 237, 268, 272, 311

Marichal, Juan, 168

Maris, Roger, 137, 138, 265, 272

Marquard, Rube, 327

Martin, Billy, 142, 205, 212

Martin, Pepper, 308

Martinez, Edgar, 261

Martinez, Pedro, 148, 170, 307

Martinez, Tino, 96, 261

Mathewson, Christy, 20, 51, 158, 320, 322

Matsui, Hideki, 128

Matsui, Kaz, 335

Matthau, Walter, 337

Matthews, Eddie, 63, 111

Mattingly, Don, 46, 89, 237, 261

Mauch, Gene, 209

Mays, Willie, 58, 129, 130, 233, 243, 258

Mazeroski, Bill, 108

McCarthy, Jack, 33, 34

McCarthy, Joe, 211

McCarver, Tim, 81, 180, 190

McCovey, Willie, 58, 96, 260, 273

McDowell, Sam, 179

McEwing, Joe, 124

McGarthy, Jack, 33, 34

McGinnity, Joe "Iron Man," 173

McGraw, John, 25, 298

McGraw, Tim, 159

McGraw, Tug, 159

McGriff, Fred, 262, 297, 301

McGwire, Mark, 98, 244, 262, 272

McKechnie, Bill, 199

McKeon, Jack, 206, 286

McLain, Denny, 170

Medwick, Joe "Ducky," 135, 216, 243

Meusel, Bob, 228

Mientkiewicz, Doug, 89

Millan, Felix, 239

Milledge, Lastings, 218, 259

Miller, Roscoe, 166

Millwood, Kevin, 160

Milwaukee Braves, 315

Milwaukee Brewers, 290

Minnesota Twins, 15, 291

Mize, Johnny, 327

Molina, Bengie, 186

Molitor, Paul, 111, 229, 234, 309

"Money player," definition of, 76

Morandini, Micky, 103

Morgan, Joe, 28, 104, 265

Morris, Mat, 56

Mota, Andy, 330

Mota, Jose, 330

Mota, Manny, 238, 330

Mueller, Bill, 238

Mulder, Mark, 12

Munson. Thurman, 14, 194

Murray, Eddie, 233, 234

Murtaugh, Danny, 296

Musial, Stan, 48, 230, 233, 245, 271

Mussina, Mike, 166

Nabors, John, 163

National Association of Baseball Players
first official rule book, 41
and National League, 39
number of teams in 1867, 45

National Baseball Hall of Fame, opening of, 18

National League
Central Division, 41
East Division, 40
first president of, 26
origin of, 39
West Division, 38

Natural, The, 337

Navajo batting games, 42, 43

Negro League World Series, first, 13

Nettles, Greg, 262

New York Highlanders, 293

New York Mets, 11, 292

New York Military Academy, 336

New York Yankees, 57, 293, 320, 325

Newark Eagles, 324

Newcombe, Don, 165

Newhouser, Hal, 156

Newsom, Bobo, 326

Niekro, Joe, 31

Niekro, Phil, 31

Nomo, Hideo, 157

Northey, Ron, 226

Norworth, Jack, 65

O'Connor, Mike, 148

O'Doul, Frank "Lefty," 217

O'Neal, Tatum, 337

O'Neill, Paul, 132

O'Reilly, Bill, 337

Oakland Athletics, 30, 294, 316

Oh, Sadahura, 135

Olerud, John, 170

Oliva, Tony, 143, 226

On deck, definition of, 80

Ortiz, David, 93, 312

Ott, Mel, 29, 130

Owen, Mickey, 191

Paciorek, John, 236

Paige, Leroy "Satchel," 27, 158

Palmeiro, Rafael, 93, 99, 232

Palmer, Jim, 169

Parker, Dave, 240

Pearce, Richard "Dickey," 83

Pearson, Albie, 275

Pena, Tony, 206

Pendleton, Terry, 218

Perez, Eduardo, 330

Perez, Tony, 33, 97, 179, 297, 330

Petrocelli, Rico, 266

Pettite, Andy, 287

Philadelphia Athletics, 30

Philadelphia Phillies, 295, 316

Philley, Dave, 278

Piazza, Mike, 184–185, 326

Pierre, Juan, 286

Piersall, Jimmy, 146, 336

Pinella, Lou, 282

Pitcher's rubber, 31

Pitchers, 147–180

Pittsburgh Alleghenys, 18

Pittsburgh Crawfords, 186

Pittsburgh Pirates, 320, 324

Pivot foot, 70

Player substitutions, first, 10

"Plunker," definition of, 76

Podsednik, Scott, 51, 290

Polo Grounds, 32, 42, 256, 292

Porter, Darrell, 183

Posada, Jorge, 190

Powell, Boog, 116, 117, 255

Pride of St. Louis, The, 335

Pride of the Yankees, The, 335

Princeton University, 213

Prior, Mark, 158

Pryor, Richard, 336

Puckett, Kirby, 144

Pujols, Albert, 13, 96, 99, 100

Quisenberry, Dan, 168

"Rabbit ears," definition of, 75

Radatz, Dick, 173

Raines, Tim, 304

"Rajah, The," 103

Ramirez, Manny, 59, 127, 143

Randa, Joe, 50

Randolph, Willie, 292

"Rapid Robert," 173

RBI, definition of, 80

Reach, Al, 66

Reagan, Ronald, 335

Redford, Robert, 337

Reese, Harold "Pee Wee," 122

Regulation baseball game, 73

Renteria, Edgar, 311

Resin bag, use of, 27

"Resolutes, The," 282

Reulbach, Ed, 160, 161

Reyes, Jose, 120, 307

"Rhubarb," definition of, 87

Richard, J.R., 166

Richardson, Bobby, 104

Rickey, Branch, 325

Ridge, Tom, 336

Rifleman, 334

Right fielder, description of, 139

Ripkin, Billy, 331

Ripkin, Cal Jr., 119, 233, 278, 331

Ripkin, Cal Sr., 331

Risberg, Charles "Swede," 55

Rivera, Mariano, 150, 167, 293

Rizzuto, Phil, 122

Robbins, Tim, 336

Robertson, Dave, 314

Robinson, Brooks, 29, 112

Robinson, Frank, 43, 126, 246, 248, 259, 278

Robinson, Jackie, 17, 253, 335

Robinson, Wilbert, 278

Rodriguez, Alex, 22, 23, 114, 239, 254, 313, 326

Rodriguez, Ivan "Pudge," 63, 183

Roe, Preacher, 167

Rogers, Kenny, 150

Rolen, Scott, 111

Rollins, Jimmy, 122

Rose, Pete, 31, 103, 229, 234

Rosen, Al, 116, 117, 259

Rothstein, Arnold, 54

Rounders, 44

Rutgers University, 57

Ruth, Babe, 32, 46, 127, 154, 172, 237, 244, 251, 264, 266, 273, 289, 306

Ryan, John, 158

Ryan, Nolan, 47, 150, 153, 174, 275, 302

Saberhagen, Bret, 288

Sabo, Chris, 110

"Sacrifice," definition of, 85

Sacrifice fly, definition of, 85

San Diego Padres, 27, 297

San Francisco Giants, 298

Sandberg, Ryne, 104, 105

Santana, Johan, 155

Santiago, Benito, 187

Santo, Ron, 216

"Say Hey Kid, The," 58, 129

Schalk, Ray, 53

Schilling, Curt, 167

Schmidt, Mike, 114, 316

Schott, Marge, 282

Schroeder, Dottie, 247

Scioscia, Mike, 199

"Scooter," 122

Seabol, Scott, 263

Seattle Mariners, 299

Seattle Pilots, 290

Seaver, Tom, 172, 174

Second basemen, 102–109

Seinfeld, 335

Selig, Bud, 313

Seton Hall University, 56

Sewell brothers, Joe, 329

Sexson, Richie, 290

Shantz, Bobby, 151

Shaw, Robert, 155

Shea Stadium 292

Sheen, Charlie, 336

Sheffield, Gary, 143, 255, 286

Shibe Park, 33

"Shoestring" catch, definition of, 86

Shortstops, 118–124

"Shot heard round the world," 257

Showalter, Buck, 302

Sierra, Ruben, 218

Sievers, Roy, 262

Simmons, Al, 240

Sisler, George, 227

Skowron, Bill, 94, 95

"Slump," definition of, 80

Smith, Ed, 15

Smith, Elmer, 59

Smith, Ozzie, 43, 118

Smoltz, John, 178, 319

Snider, Duke, 130, 244, 259, 267, 327

Somerset Patriots, 151

Soriano, Alfonso, 104, 317

Sosa, Sammy, 56, 131, 138, 224, 267

Spahn, Warren, 253

Speaker, Tris, 140, 231, 234, 283

Spencer, Daryl, 298

Spencer, Shane, 180

Spitball, 28

"Squeeze play," description of, 83

"Squib," definition of, 76

Stargell, Willie, 58, 90, 246

Staub, Rusty, 236, 268

Steinbach, Terry, 194

Steinbrenner, George, 326

Stengel, Casey, 66, 140, 181, 192, 200, 201, 211

St. Louis Cardinals, 51, 300, 314

St. Louis Perfectos, 51

Stolen bases, statistics on, 62

Stone, Toni, 102

Stuart, Dick, 94, 95

Suicide squeeze play, 188–189

Sullivan, Joe "Sport," 54

Sunday baseball games, origin of, 87

Sutter, Bruce, 149

Sutton, Don, 160, 161, 174

Suzuki, Ichiro, 46, 126, 227, 299

Sweeney, Mark, 313, 314

"Switch hitter," definition of, 82

Taft, William Howard, 25

"Take Me Out to the Ball Game," 65

Tampa Bay Devil Rays 31, 301

Tanner, Chuck, 325

Tatis, Fernando, 224, 225

Tejada, Miguel, 120

Templeton, Garry, 123

Tenace, Gene, 193, 294

Terry, Bill, 221, 298

Terry, Ralph, 167

"Texas Leaguer," definition of, 76

Texas Rangers, 10, 302, 334

Third basemen, 110–115

Thomas, Frank, 94, 95, 242

Thome, Jim, 90, 267

Thompson, Bobby, 257

3,000 hit club, 229–235

Throneberry, Marv, 100

Tobin, Jack, 216

Toney, Fred, 152

Torborg, Jeff, 213

Toronto Blue Jays, 30, 303

Torre, Joe, 18, 97, 190, 198, 205, 207, 258

Traynor, Harold "Pie," 59

"Triple," definition of, 85

Tripleheader, first, 18

Triple play
    definition of, 75
    unassisted, 39, 99, 103, 107, 118

Trump, Donald, 336

Turnstiles, origin of, 87

Tyng, Jim, 9

Unassisted triple play, odds of, 39

Utility men, 124

Utley, Chase, 308

Valenin, Jose, 224

Valentin, Javier, 186

Valentin, John, 118

Valentin, Jose, 186

Van Cleef, Ray, 57

Vance, Dazzy, 63

VanderMeer, Johnny, 175

Varitek, Jason, 61, 280

Vaughn, Hippo, 152

Vaughn, Mo, 56

Ventura, Robin, 34, 110

Vernon, Mickey, 226

Versalles, Zoilo, 116, 117

Virdon, Bill, 205

Waddel, Rube, 176

Wagner, Butts, 329

Wagner, Honus, 119, 216, 234, 329

Waite, Charles, 27

Walker, Larry, 134, 284

Walters, Bucky, 165

Wambsganss, William, 106, 107

Waner, Paul, 138, 234, 296

Washington Nationals, 304

Watson, Bob, 48, 247

Weathers, David, 178

Weaver, Earl, 202

Weaver, George "Buck," 53, 54, 115

Weaver, Joanne, 253

Wells, David, 157

Wheat, Mack, 329

Wheat, Zach, 329

White, Will, 44

Widmark, Richard, 334

Wigginton, Ty, 124

Wilhelm, Hoyt, 175

Williams College, 67

Williams, Bernie, 56, 237

Williams, Claude "Lefty," 53, 54

Williams, Dick, 203, 294

Williams, Matt, 267

Williams, Ted, 46, 64, 136, 221, 240, 243, 254, 269, 273

Willis, Dontrelle, 153

Wills, Maury, 120, 122

Wilson, Hack, 49, 135, 240

Wilson, Preston, 286

Wilson, Willie, 36, 228, 288

Wiltse, George, 162

Winfield, Dave, 137, 231

Winning Team, The, 335

Wise, Rick, 270

"Wizard of Oz, The," 43

Womack, Tony, 276

Wood, Kerry, 172

Woodling, Gene, 115

Wright, David, 11, 110, 307, 324

Wrigley Field, 59

Wrigley, Phil, 280

Wynn, Early, 163

Wynn, Jim, 269

Yastrzemski, Carl, 132, 141, 226, 229, 231, 242, 271

Yeager, Steve, 113

"Yogi," 44

Young, Chris, 171

Young, Cy, 49, 154, 168

Young, Delmon, 31

Young, Eric, 284

Young, Michael, 322

Youngblood, Joel, 239

Zeile, Todd, 89, 190, 238

Zimmer, Don, 297

Zito, Barry, 160

★ ABOUT THE AUTHOR ★

Michael J. Pellowski comes from a baseball family. His son Martin was an All-Star pitcher with an outstanding curve ball. His son Morgan was an excellent second baseman who could hit with power. His daughter Melanie was an All-Area Shortstop in softball. His son Matt was a homerun-hitting third baseman.

Michael J. Pellowski himself was an All-Star centerfielder in high school. He went to Rutgers University in New Jersey on a football scholarship and captained the 1970 team while winning All-East honors. He went on to have pro trials in the CFL and NFL. At Rutgers, he also won three letters in baseball. In the days before metal bats and the DH, he posted a career batting average of .312 and once had seven consecutive pinch hits.